I0661394

William Douglas MacKenzie

Christianity and the Progress of Man

As Illustrated by Modern Missions

William Douglas MacKenzie

Christianity and the Progress of Man
As Illustrated by Modern Missions

ISBN/EAN: 9783337026615

Printed in Europe, USA, Canada, Australia, Japan

Cover: Foto ©Lupo / pixelio.de

More available books at **www.hansebooks.com**

CHRISTIANITY

AND THE

PROGRESS OF MAN

AS ILLUSTRATED BY MODERN MISSIONS

BY

W. DOUGLAS MACKENZIE, M.A

PROFESSOR IN CHICAGO THEOLOGICAL SEMINARY

EDINBURGH & LONDON

OLIPHANT ANDERSON & FERRIER

1898

DEDICATED

TO

MY FATHER, JOHN MACKENZIE

AND

ELLEN MACKENZIE, MY MOTHER

WHO HAVE LABOURED TOGETHER AS

MISSIONARIES OF JESUS CHRIST

IN

SOUTH AFRICA

FOR

THE PAST FORTY YEARS

PREFACE

WE begin to speak with increasing frequency of the characteristic events and changes of the nineteenth century, as it draws rapidly to its close. Two of the greatest facts—I ought to say *the* two greatest facts—are undoubtedly the unification of the race and the establishment of the Christian religion as a working force among nearly all nations. The two facts are closely related both in nature and history. How the one universalistic religion has been moulding the life of the one race of mankind during the nineteenth century—that is the subject of this little book.

My obligations to friends and authors are numerous. The works to which I owe most are the great missionary biographies of Dr. George Smith, the remarkable " Report of the Missionary Conference, London, 1888 " (which I cite by the abbreviation " L. M. C."), and Mr. Edwin Hodder's comprehensive history of modern missions, entitled "The Conquests of the Cross."   Of course there is a large amount of missionary literature to which I am indebted which it is needless to specify.

W. D. M.

March 1898.

CONTENTS

CHRISTIANITY

AND THE

PROGRESS OF MAN

CHAPTER I

INTRODUCTION

THE aim of the following chapters may be briefly described thus. We have seen in recent years a revival of interest in the problem of religion. Books and essays have appeared which indicate that the superficial judgment of, say, twenty years ago, which relegated religion to the region of the superstitious and the irrational, is being abandoned. The mood has changed. Few people now think that religion, that the Christian religion, can be removed from the field of intellectual discussion without serious injury to other departments of science and philosophy. This change of attitude is due to various influences, of which I shall name three.

On the one hand, we find that the over-confidence of the Positivists and the Agnostics has disappeared.

Their philosophy is not final. Their characteristic
theories of knowledge, of evolution, of reality,
have by no means solved the problems presented
by human nature and history. Their failure
suggests to many minds the idea that, after all,
the assertions of the Christian religion at which
they were wont to gird most vigorously may be
true. At anyrate, not one of these fundamental
assertions has been really disproved. On the
other hand, the deeper study of the history of man
is making more apparent every day the profound,
nay, the organic place which religion occupies in
the evolution of society. This is one result of
the Science of Comparative Religion, especially as
it reveals its almost constant and intricate relations
with the evolution of society, and hence with the
still inchoate Science of Sociology, whose object is
to understand that evolution. Even Mr. Herbert
Spencer recognises this, and traces many mistakes
in sociological reasonings to the influence of the
"anti-theological bias." "Ignoring the truth for
which religions stand," he says, "it (this bias)
undervalues religious institutions in the past,
thinks they are useless in the present, and expects
they will leave no representatives in the future."[1]
Mr. Benjamin Kidd, too, has done good service
by the vigorous protest which he enters against
the folly of neglecting the study of religion as
a "true cause" in social evolution. In the third
place, this change of attitude regarding religion
seems to be accounted for largely by the ardour

[1] *The Study of Sociology*, p. 312.

with which the Church of Christ has extended
and deepened its influence during this century.
We have before us a spectacle which, looked at
from any point of view, must be called sublime.
From being on the whole a European religion,
Christianity has begun in this century to deserve
the name of "world religion." In Great Britain
and America it appears to be as vigorous, and as
thorough in its influence as ever it was. There it
is coping with forces which never before met it in
such power and intensity. They are the creation
of that freedom of thought, that freedom of action,
that marvellous development of industry, and its
correlative passion for amusement and recreation,
which characterise especially the English-speaking world, and which in their combination are
paralleled in no earlier period of history. If the
Church seems to have lost its hold on some sections
of society, it has yet more than maintained its own
life of faith and its determination to penetrate all
industry and politics and recreation with the spirit
of Jesus Christ. A temporary and partial "set-
back," which must be admitted, is being made the
occasion for a stronger exertion of its characteristic forces. Few will be inclined to affirm that
at any earlier time the masses of the people manifested more of *intelligent* faith in the gospel, or
more of the *spirit* of Jesus Christ in their social
and political ideals, however much there may be
yet to attain.

But, after all, it is in the work of Foreign
Missions that the Church has done most to prove

its social influence. For Christianity is now at work practically in every land. Amongst rude savages and under the shadow of hoary Oriental institutions it is seeking to establish itself. And its success has been so remarkable, its religious and social influence so undeniable, that every thoughtful man who has rejected its claims is bound, in the mere name of his intellectual integrity, to pause and face the facts afresh.

But, if religion holds an organic place in the evolution of society, do we not have before us an opportunity for studying its influence which no other generation may enjoy in the same way? We can see with our own eyes a superior religion as it comes in upon lower forms of social organisation, abolishes their evils, corrects their defects, and begins the development of all that is best in the ripest forms of civilisation. In ordinary conditions, where a religion, whether Christianity or any other, has been long established, its influence is more subtle and more intricate; it is less easy to separate out the actual effects, good or bad, of the religion itself from those produced by collateral causes. But in the phenomena presented by Christian missions the student of sociology has the task wonderfully simplified. He can watch the transformations of society, as they proceed with a rapidity which Europe has not seen since the third and fourth centuries. Even at that time the European tribes and nations did not move so fast towards Christian ideals of society as many in other regions are moving to-day; for then there did not exist a Church with eighteen hundred years of experience, to make it strong and clear and wise in the avoidance of dangers, and in the pursuit of its true goal along paths which are safe for Church and State. The gathered wisdom and power of all these centuries is now being concentrated by the Church upon the deliverance of all tribes and races out of barbarism into the possession of Christian institutions. This is true even though we believe that the Church is by no means yet perfected in wisdom, and that not all its representatives abroad are worthy of its ideal.

In the following pages an attempt is made to outline the kind of facts which belong to the history of missions in the nineteenth century, and which throw light upon the action of Christianity among heathen and Moslem peoples. Briefly put, the argument runs in this way. We find that Christianity, when compared with other religions, is the only one which is inherently capable of becoming universal. It is worth while to inquire into those elements in the religion of Revelation which fit it to be the religion of the race, and which are steadily moulding history towards that end (Chapter II.). During the nineteenth century this capacity has been put to the test among almost every people upon earth, and in competition with every form and grade of social and religious organisation. What is called the "missionary movement" is the means through which the battle is carried on. The result is, that we see this religious impulse occupying not the

2

sole but the supreme place in the work of unifying the race, and exalting the conditions of life. This is done by the pioneer work of the missionary (Chapter III.); by the marvellous process of Bible translation, through which one universal basis and permanent standard of religious experience is being given to all mankind (Chapter IV.); by popular education, which is provided always as a necessary part of the missionary movement, which thus springs from the religious impulse, and is sustained by the peculiar ideals of the Christian religion (Chapter V.); by the influence of that noble spirit of self-sacrifice for benevolent ends which is the unique possession of this religion, which lies at the root of self-discipline and reaches its sublime expression in martyrdom (Chapter VI.); by the immediate effect which conversion to Christ begins to produce upon personal character, family relationship, and thus upon social life and civilisation (Chapter VII.); by the influence which the Christian system exerts upon preceding religions of all kinds, rebuking and gradually putting to an end what is false or incomplete, inept or perilous, and glorifying whatsoever is true and healthful and inspiring (Chapter VIII.). In these chapters it is necessary to assert from various points of view one fact, which, however, needs to be specially emphasised. It is this. The processes, influences, or results of Christian missions cannot be understood or explained without taking continual account of the purely religious element or purpose which underlies them all. The missionary avowedly goes

as a saviour, to bring men into that which is the
central feature of Christianity, viz., the experience
of personal fellowship with God through faith in
the Saviour, Jesus Christ. The missionary and the
convert, of every age and clime, assert that the
personal and the social effects described above *only
follow this experience*; and on this momentous
affirmation Apostolic Christianity is at one with
the young Church of Polynesia, Africa, and Asia
to-day (Chapter IX.). In the last chapter I try
to draw out and summarise the significance of the
movement which has thus been described. The
progress of man is a phrase not easy to define, but
it represents something real, and Christianity
appears to be intimately bound up with it. It
must be possible to dissipate some of the vagueness
which generally envelopes our idea of human
progress, and to state some of its elements. It must
be also possible to set down some of the main
characteristics of the influence which the one
universal religion is exercising upon the race of
mankind. And perhaps this view of the interdependence of human progress and the Christian
faith may help us to decide whether that faith is
false or true (Chapter X.).

There is one matter connected with the following chapters to which I must briefly refer. It will
be noticed that little or nothing is said about the
faults and failures of individual missions and
missionaries; and some may imagine it to be
suggested that there have been none. That would,
of course, be absurd. I can adopt the language of

Bishop Westcott when he says: "I will admit to the full the fewness, the weakness, the errors, the frailties, if you please, of the workers." But the Bishop also says: "When I see the results which have been produced, I am startled, touched, humbled by the wholly disproportionate magnitude of what has been done when compared with the means which have been used to effect it." The fact is, that missionaries have manifested various degrees of ability, devotion, diligence, piety, self - sacrifice. Some have possessed elements of disposition and character, and defects of training, which either prevented or lessened the success of their work. A few have proved to be total failures. The same things must be said about individual converts from heathenism and the churches which they form. Some of the complaints which travellers and others make concerning the imperfect character of many native Christians, are no doubt founded upon actual failure on the part of the latter to manifest the pure spirit of Jesus Christ. The Apostle Paul found the same facts in the churches of Galatia and Corinth.

There are two classes of men whom one finds emphasising these defects and failures. The one class consists of shallow scoffers at missions, and even at Christianity; the other class consists of earnest Christians who view defect and failure, among missionaries and converts alike, as a dishonour to the name of Jesus Christ. But the man who desires to treat the matter scientifically has no right to be influenced by this strange concurrence in opinion of opposing classes of men. Neither the hackneyed superficialities of the scoffer nor the spiritual criticisms of the saint ought to influence our judicial estimate of the actual work done by the Christian religion. Christianity never professed to be a force working in a vacuum. It is a force among forces, suffering friction, reaction, and direct collision of all kinds. Hence the history of its effects must include, as Church History confessedly does, the record of many fierce conflicts, of periods when movement was slow, of periods when there seemed to be an arrest of progress, as well as of periods when advance was rapid and triumphant. But no student of evolution would maintain that the signs and incidents of the struggle for existence lessen the significance of the survival of the fittest. Rather would he consider that they help to emphasise the inherent vitality of that form of life which has triumphed. It is the aim of these pages to describe what the missionary movement has actually achieved, to emphasise the positive aspects of the warfare which is going on between human nature and the forces of this wondrous fact called the Gospel of Jesus Christ. In the closing chapter something will be said regarding the conditions which render its progress gradual, and hence any one of its stages in the individual or in the community both morally and spiritually imperfect.

In attempting to present the evidence for my conclusions in the following chapters, nothing like a full account of the facts has been aimed at. To describe the phenomena of missionary experience with anything like completeness would require the prolonged labours of a specialist in this wide and ever-extending field.[1]   My aim has been to draw illustrations from various countries and the work of various societies.   These illustrations are not to be considered as in themselves alone affording final proof ; they derive their evidential strength from the fact that they are typical.   No one incident or experience in these pages stands alone in the history of modern missions.   Each might be easily multiplied over and over again, and most could be multiplied a hundred or a thousand times by any one who cared to scan the pages of magazines, reports, and books, with that end in view.

In order to make the mass of evidence which lies behind the arguments from missionary experience appear in its true proportions, the reader should keep the following facts in mind : —

1. As to the geographical extent of missionary operations.   Dr. George Smith several years ago said that there were " five great regions of the

---

[1] Since these chapters were written, I have been allowed to see the proof-sheets of part of a work which exactly answers the description suggested above.   It is entitled *Christian Missions and Social Progress*. (Oliphant, Anderson & Ferrier.)   The author, the Rev. J. S. Dennis, D.D., is indeed a specialist in this department, and has spared neither time, energy, nor expense to make his work as complete as possible.   The bibliographies attached to the various chapters are extensive, the summation of facts elaborate, and the tables of statistics with which the second volume is to conclude will certainly be the most exhaustive which have appeared in relation to the work of foreign missions.

world as yet totally unreached by the missionary." [1] These are Thibet and High Asia, Arabia, the Soudan, Amazonia, Russia in Asia. Now this statement means that, if we subtract these regions, the rest of the world is open to, and is being occupied with great rapidity by, the missionary agencies. China is not, of course, adequately occupied, nor India, nor Africa. But these portions of the world are open, and in them missionary effort is steadily spreading year by year. No one doubts that in a few years all the lands named by Dr. George Smith, except Russia in Asia, will be penetrated by evangelical missionaries.

2. Nor is the army of workers merely sporadic. However inadequate it may be, when compared with the work which has yet to be done, no one can fail to be impressed by its vast extent when considered in itself, and in relation to the short period of one hundred years during which it has grown. One writer puts the matter thus: "Christendom is represented in heathendom by about 11,450 Europeans and Americans of both sexes. Of these about 4300 are ordained, something less than 1000 are unordained, 3650 are wives, and 2575 are unmarried women. With these are associated 4200 ordained and 43,000 unordained natives, toiling as pastors, evangelists, teachers, etc. The entire missionary force numbers not far from 55,000." [2]

[1] In *Missions at Home and Abroad*, p. 146.
[2] *A Hundred Years of Missions*, by Rev. D. L. Leonard (Funk and Wagnalls), p. 417.

According to Dr. Vahl, one of the leading authorities on missionary statistics, the following were the figures for the year 1893 : [1]—There were in existence 331 missionary societies and committees whose work was that of evangelising the heathen. Their income amounted to $12,397,605. There were 5638 missionaries, the majority being married, and 2893 unmarried female missionaries. Of native workers there were 4074 ministers and 49,718 helpers.

This great force is everywhere working for the same ends, by the same means, under the same inspiration.

[1] *Missions to the Heathen in* 1892 *and* 1893 : *A Statistical Review.* Copenhagen : Fr. Berthelsen.

CHAPTER II

RELIGION is the main fact through whose influence the spirit of man becomes released from selfishness or individualism. It is true that patriotism has exerted a remarkable power of this kind upon the minds of the world's citizens; thrilling heroism is found in the annals of most peoples, certainly of all those who have contributed anything of value to the history of mankind. And, indeed, patriotism and religion were for long almost synonymous terms. But selfishness is not really being eradicated from the human heart until some force is at work which so exalts men that they become interested in man as man. Patriotism in its noblest forms in Athens and Babylon, in Carthage and Rome, always resulted in contempt for the rest of the world. To be a foreigner was to be a barbarian, fit only for conquest, tribute and slavery. Hence patriotism, where it has been unreleased from its narrowness by a wider religious outlook, has been an incentive not only to sublime self-sacrifice, but also to the utmost cruelty and oppression. For a moment a Latin poet might catch a vision of the worth of mankind as such, and sweep a Roman audience into enthusiasm by his vigorous expression of the rare conception—"Nihil humanum a me alienum puto." Or, again, a man like Socrates might call himself a citizen of the world. But these moments of illumination were extremely rare; not only rare—they were also purely personal. Neither philosophy nor poetry could make them the heritage of the common mind and a working force in human society. It needed that which religion alone can give, viz., the higher view of God and of every man's relations to Him, to dignify man before the eyes of men.

But religion itself has had many forms and degrees in the history of man. Not all of these were by any means adapted to have a share in the work of liberalising man's thought of man. When the religious spirit was still so impoverished as to think of the god of a people or a tribe as being merely a local deity, religion became identified with patriotism in the work of developing tribal and national selfishness. It needed the advent of what have been called the world-religions to lift man to the view-point from which the true dignity of man could become a reality for the practical life. This was in part attained, for example, in Buddha, and possibly in Confucius. But the fact is, that the teaching of these men, being disconnected from a definite doctrine of God and from the conception of a future life, could only retain the interest and

affection of the masses of men, by becoming associated with the ordinary faith of the people in the
existence of the gods and a future sphere of rewards
and punishments.   Nevertheless, in their systems
there was so real a perception of the deeper moral
obligations between man and man as such, and, at
at least in Buddha, of the relations between
practical morality and spiritual or religious vision
and experience, that a partial foundation was laid
for a certain kind of interest in humanity.   Then
it was that men found themselves under a sense of
obligation to deliver to others the truths which
had been made known to themselves, and religious
missions arose.   Not now as a part of patriotism,
not now in the interest of the tribe by means of
war, did the Buddha and his successors make known
his rules and advocate his views, but because they
had come to see, if but dimly, a little of what man
is and of what man ought to be.   Both Confucianism
and Buddhism failed either to maintain the original
high convictions of their founders, or to release
themselves from the corruptions of idolatry in
which they so speedily became entangled; and
they lost their first glory and elevating power.

It was reserved for the religion of Revelation to
attain true and permanent universality.   It first
established among men those views of God and
man, which first made the world of men loom up
as one race with one greatest and deepest need,
and so created what we called distinctively the
missionary movement.   And this sublime power
it derived from the fact that those views were

not any longer the mere theories or dreams or
aspirations of the human heart seeking God, but
proceeded from the acts of the divine heart seeking
man.   The new conceptions of human nature were
derived from those conditions of fellowship with
Himself, which the living God, in the course of
revelation, historically established and made possible
for all men.   In its earlier stage this religion of
Revelation was indeed confined to one people; in
connection with the history of that one people it
passed from the simplest stages, in the beliefs of
the desert tribes who found themselves in covenant
with Jehovah, to the lofty apprehension of the
nature and being of God, represented, say, in the
Book of Isaiah, to the deep and rich spiritual experiences reflected alike in Psalmist and Prophet.   Even
the development of the idea of sacrifice and ritual
in the worship of Israel may instruct us concerning
the steps by which deepening awe of the living
God, and deepening dread of sinful relations to
Him, led the conscience of Israel to seek more and
more adequate means of expression, and a more
inward reconciliation with Him.   It is a common
but a serious mistake to suppose that this religion
of the Old Testament, because concerned immediately with the chosen people, was therefore narrow
and exclusive.   It is true that it made use of the
national spirit, and even strengthened and emphasised that spirit; it is true that at certain periods
prophetism laid great emphasis upon the necessity
for maintaining a policy of separation from all
other tribes and peoples, with their idolatrous

customs and degraded habits. But it must be remembered that this was demanded, just in order that Israel might be preserved for its unique and sublime function in the world. And it must be also remembered that this insistence upon the isolation of Israel was not felt even by the prophets to be inconsistent with the idea that ultimately Israel would come to have the utmost significance for all peoples.

If we ask how it was that the religion of Israel came to possess this element of universalism, and to be fitted as the precursor of the one only religion which is actually and fully universalistic, the answer will direct our attention to three aspects of Old Testament teaching. First, there is the doctrine of God. Israel no doubt began with a very simple and even crude idea of Jehovah. Very probably they spoke of Him just as neighbouring peoples spoke of their gods, and for a long time their forms of altar service may have been quite indistinguishable by any fundamental feature from those of kindred tribes. But Israel came to feel and to see that Jehovah is the living God ; that the universal God had laid hold of their national life and history and connected His self-revelation with their fortunes and attainments. The result has vindicated their faith. He who was known to Israel as Jehovah, was and is the God of all ages and of all men. It was only gradually, " at sundry times and in divers manners," that God spoke to Israel " by the prophets." But He verily did speak, and the Old Testament contains, from its first page

to its last, many marvellous statements regarding
Him. The main facts which we learn are that
God is the one and only God; that He created the
world; that though the nations worshipped other
gods, they were false or unreal gods; that Jehovah
alone lives, and He is the God of all; that He hates
iniquity and loves righteousness; that He has
chosen Israel, His servant, but that He has done
this in order that at last all nations may call
themselves blessed, on account of and through
Israel. .

Second, there is the doctrine of man. Mankind
is regarded even in the Old Testament as being one
race. The division between one section of the
race and another, between Asiatic and Ethiopian
for instance, is traced not to a difference of origin,
but to the action of divine providence. The very
differences of language which to the heathen world
seemed so mysterious were accounted for, to the
thought of Israel, by attributing them to the
judicial wrath of God. But all such differences are
almost superficial. Men are all one before Jehovah,
who created all, who is the actual Master of all,
and who will yet vindicate His indefeasible rights
and His universal authority.[1] Although man feels
himself lowly and of no account when he thinks of
Jehovah, who has set His glory above the heavens,
yet, when he sees his own place in nature, man feels
that upon humanity itself there rests a peculiar
dignity; he is "crowned with glory and honour."[2]
Man belongs to a double system, for he is capable

[1] Gen. i. 1-11.   [2] Ps. viii. 5.

not only of beholding and appreciating the wisdom and might of God, as displayed in the outward universe, but of turning to another which is no less real and infinitely more precious. This is the world of moral and spiritual law, the realm where man moves in personal relations with God.[1]

Third, the Old Testament record of Revelation contains that great doctrine of a Messiah and a Messianic salvation. The Israelite pictures Abraham as having received an assurance that the dealings of God with him would be significant for all nations. And indeed throughout these Scriptures we find many references not only to the attitude of grace which God sustains towards the heathen world,[2] but to the definite purpose which He had, to reach through Israel to all the nations. It is true indeed, as has been said, that "it belonged essentially to the idea of God prevalent among his countrymen that the Israelite should claim the whole earth as the kingdom of his God."[3] But this idea of the universal relation of God to all men becomes specially developed in connection with the hope of a Messianic age. This hope assumed various forms under the divine guidance, these forms being largely determined by the moral and religious condition and the political problems of the generation to which a prophet spoke or out of which a psalmist sang. In a very large number of cases the promise of that final boon, that com-

---

[1] Cf. Pss. xix., cxxxix. ; Isa. xl. 12–31 ; Prov. viii. 22–36, etc.

[2] Isa. xix. 18–22 ; Mal. i. 11 (R.V.).

[3] Riehm's *Messianic Prophecy* (Trans.), p. 92.

pleted national blessedness to Israel, was made to
sweep also the other nations within its influence.
Hence the perfect King, who is described so glori-
ously in the Seventy-second Psalm, who is to rule
over the whole known world, is to be served and
blessed by "all nations."

Even that strange conception of the mountain of
the Lord, to which in Isaiah so much reference is
made, which is pictured as being reared in the
Holy City, is to be like a magnet drawing the
nations·unto it.[1]   Jehovah shall lift up a signal for
the nations, and the feast of fat things which He
provides shall be unto all peoples.[2]   "And He shall
annihilate in this mountain the covering which
covereth all peoples, and the web which is woven
over all nations."[3]   In the second book of Isaiah
these references to the universal significance of the
Messiah and His kingdom become still more clear
and more impressive.   It is true that even in the
loftiest of these we find that special note of patriotism still ringing strong and clear, which expected
that in the golden age to come the world would
be subject to Israel, and Israel would be exalted
to an actual lordship over the nations.[4]   But there
are occasions when the conception is distinctly
subordinated to the religious and spiritual hope
of seeing mankind redeemed.   It was not till
the New Covenant was actually established that
the last vibration of the ancient tone of narrow

[1] Isa. ii. 2, 3.   [2] Isa. xi. 12 ; xxv. 6.
[3] Isa. xxv. 7, 8 (Professor Cheyne's Trans.).
[4] Isa. lx. 3, 9, 10–16 ; lxii. 1, 2.

patriotism was stilled, and the mere blessing of man as man contemplated as the supreme issue of all history.

At last, however, in Christianity itself the true religion was finally established and freed from all artificial restrictions and national limitations. Then the true world-religion appeared among men, and began that marvellous redemptive and educative process which to-day it is carrying on more widely and more powerfully than in any earlier age.

This universalism we should expect to find in the Gospels, of course; for, if in the life and work of our Lord Himself it does not appear, we should find it difficult to resist the argument that it was an addition to His gospel made by Paul and certain other apostles in after days. But an addition to the gospel can never hold our allegiance, however high its authority, half so powerfully as that which belongs to its very nature and essence. Now when we examine the Gospels, we are, perhaps, surprised to find that Jesus makes hardly any explicit references to the world at large, or to the universal range of the revelation which He has brought into the world. He does, indeed, say once, "The field is the world";[1] and twice He speaks of His disciples in like manner, saying: "Ye are the salt of the earth"; "Ye are the light of the world."[2] Once, in describing the kingdom of God, He says explicitly: "They shall come from the east and the west, and from the north and the south, and shall sit down in the kingdom of God";[3]

[1] Matt. xiii. 38.   [2] Matt. v. 13, 14.   [3] Luke xiii. 29.

3

and He speaks of the final judgment, "when the Son of man shall come in His glory," as an hour when "before Him shall be gathered all the nations."[1] The Fourth Gospel seems to attribute to Him the glorious universal affirmation, "God so loved the world, that He gave His only begotten Son, that whosoever believeth on Him should not perish, but have everlasting life"; and again records that He said: "I, if I be lifted up from the earth, will draw all men unto me."[2]

But, after all, the deepest and most impressive feature of this universalism of the gospel of Christ is not to be found in these few incidental expressions which fell from His lips; it lies rather in the very gospel which made them so appropriate and natural that they seem incidental, and in themselves inadequate to account for the world-wide reach of His authority to-day. While He restricted His personal ministry and the missionary activity of His disciples during His lifetime to Israel, we yet feel that in doing so He was conscious of a deliberate act of self-restraint; that He was aware of a seeming contradiction between the substance of His gospel and the range within which alone He made it known. There are recorded words of His which seem to bring this element of His consciousness to the surface.[3] "As He was willing to be the corn of wheat cast into the ground to die . . . so, He was willing to be God's minister

---

[1] Matt. xxv. 32.   [2] John iii. 16 ; xii. 32.

[3] Matt. x. 5, 6, 23 ; xv. 24–28 ; Mark xii. 9 ; xiii. 10 ; xiv. 9 ; John xii. 20.

to the Jews, as the best preparation for a future ministry among the Gentiles."[1] The real source of the universalism of the gospel is in the gospel itself. That gospel is the Christ Himself. He is both the messenger and the message of God. Through Him men come to know the Father. When a man gives up all to follow Him, that man begins to have eternal life. The Father's love reaches the world through the Son. Man receives the assurance of the forgiveness of sins, of fellowship with God, through Him, the Son of man, who is appointed Son of God and Saviour of the world. Now throughout the elucidation of this gospel by means of His words concerning both God and man, as well as by His deeds of power and of self-sacrifice, the fact becomes more and more evident that no national conditions whatsoever belong to the new experience which is being created for mankind in and through the Son of man. While He restricts His outward presence to Israel and His movements almost wholly to Galilee and Judea, His appeal is ever made to man, His gospel is for man. This will appear most clearly from a consideration of two chief features in His teaching and work.

First, there is His manifestation alike in word and work of the grace of God. On His first Messianic visit to Nazareth He referred to the fact that even in the Old Testament there were signs of the kindness of God towards those who were outside the covenant;[2] and through all His

---

[1] *The Kingdom of God*, by Professor Bruce, p. 57.
[2] Luke iv. 25–27.

ministry He strives to make it plain that divine
grace is effectual unto all who are lost, and,
therefore, it would seem, breaks down all national
and artificial barriers. He never connects the
bestowal of salvation with any conditions except
with those which are possible to all men, viz.,
faith and repentance. Ritual has no place in His
conception of worship. A Samaritan may worship
the Father as truly as a Jew.[1] A Samaritan may
show an obedience to God superior to that of either
Levite or Priest.[2] Wherever there is conscious
need, the grace of God is active. Even publicans,
who have become worse than mere Gentiles, who
are guilty indeed of a kind of apostasy in acting
as tax-gatherers for the Roman Empire, may enter
into the kingdom of God.

Second, in correlation with the grace of God
as the only fountain of salvation, there is the
faith of man as its only channel. The divine grace
is a transforming force, and faith is its instrument.
Now, Jesus Christ was the first teacher, in the
history of the world and of the world's religions,
who swept all other considerations aside and
made faith the sole and indispensable ground of
fellowship with God. His dealings with men
in this regard are more powerful evidence than
any set exposition of justification by faith from
His lips could have been. Righteousness He does
demand, obedience full and free. But it is obedience to God apprehended as the Father; it is
obedience to the words of Jesus; it is the service

[1] John iv. 21–24.   [2] Luke x. 33.

of man, even unto the bearing of the cross, "for My sake." That is to say, before there can be obedience or service, there must be faith. Before there can be true worship of God as Spirit, He must be named as Father; and before or in that act there must be faith. All men are capable of faith as soon as they begin to hear of Jesus the Christ and to feel their need of boons which God can give through Him. The publicans and harlots, the Gentile centurion, the Syrophœnician woman, the Samaritans who receive Him, are all equally welcome to His love and to the blessings which He can bestow; for they show themselves capable of faith towards Him as "the Sent" of God. This gospel of Jesus, this announcement of a fellowship with God whose only conditions on the manward side are repentance and faith, this is a gospel for a world of lost men and women. At its heart it is universal, because it reveals God face to face with every man, and it bids every man look up and see that face of love.

All this becomes clearer still, after the death and resurrection have taken place. Then the gospel becomes in fullest manner what it had not been before, a working force in human hearts. We sometimes speak as if the words of Jesus interpret the meaning of His death and resurrection. But to the apostolic experience the opposite was the case. It was the crucifixion, and the victory that followed it, which interpreted His ministry and His words. Then His gospel became intelligible, then His influence attained a new glory. Then they were begotten again unto a living hope, and knew that Jesus was the Christ, the Son of God, and that they had reconciliation with God through faith in Him.[1] Then also those who stood around Him ere He ascended heard Him say: "Go ye into all the world and preach the gospel to the whole creation."[2] They only gradually came to apprehend the universal meaning of all this. Unto Peter this revelation came when he was sent to Cornelius and saw the Holy Spirit produce on heathen men the same external signs which had resulted from His descent upon those who were Jews. Then the Pauline ministry began, and Paul came to see that, when the Jews rejected and the Gentiles accepted Christ and received the Holy Spirit, the gospel of justification by faith carried with it the abolition of all race and sex and class distinctions.[3] "God is no respecter of persons," both Peter and Paul exclaimed. But it was Paul who grasped the significance of it most deeply. To the churches of Galatia, made up both of Jews and Gentiles, he says: "There can be neither Jew nor Greek; there can be neither bond nor free; there can be no male and female; for ye are all one man in Christ Jesus." To the Corinthians he says: "Unto them that are called, both Jews and Greeks, Christ the power of God and the wisdom of God." To the Romans he says that the gospel of Christ "is the power of God unto salvation to every one that believeth, to the Jew first, and

---

[1] 1 Pet. i. 3 ; John xx. 31.
[2] Matt. xxviii. 18, 19; Mark xvi. 15.   [3] Gal. iii. 26–28.

also to the Gentile." [1] Writing to the Colossians
from his Roman prison, the great apostle explains
that the barriers which had separated Jew and
Gentile have been destroyed "through the blood of
His cross." That one life of Jesus Christ, the Son
of God, who gave Himself in sacrifice for the sins of
many, belonged to no one race, but to all. The
virtue of His person and work cannot be limited
by aught save the unbelief of those who reject Him.
This unbelief turns His grace into "a savour of death
unto death" to themselves. This great wonder,
Christ in a man, "the hope of glory," is the glorious
secret which God has kept so long hid from ages
and from generations, for inscrutable but divine
reasons, which now at last is laid open for all men.
It is to be made known among the Gentiles, "that
we may present every man perfect in Christ
Jesus."

Here then at last is a religion which is for the
world. It has the fullest consciousness of the
terrors of the Lord; it faces the awful majesty of
His holy name; it knows as no other religion what
horror and shame are wrapped up in that word sin.
It confronts the weakness of man and his unworthiness as frankly and fully as is conceivable. And
yet it gives to man an experience of personal
fellowship, of living reconciliation with God. It
announces to man the individual love of God for
every man; it assures him of this love by pointing
to the cross of Christ and the glory of Easter
morning; it calls on him to love and trust God in

[1] Gal. iii. 28 ; 1 Cor. i. 24 ; Rom. i. 16 (R. V.).

Jesus Christ.   It lays down no conditions regarding
the kind of sins a man has committed in the past,
or the rank in life, or the tribe or nation, into which
he was born.   Wherever the Word goes, it goes to
man as man, to the weak as weak, to the strong as
strong, to the lost as lost.   It summons him to life,
life with God, life in God, life for God through
faith in Jesus Christ.

Very speedily the religion of Christ was spread
through the known world.   Within the first four
or five· centuries it had conquered the Roman
Empire.   From Constantinople to Spain and from
Asia Minor to the west side of India, from Britain
to the Sahara Desert and on to Abyssinia, the
Church had extended its influence, and the life of
fellowship with God had been received by those
who believed in Jesus Christ.   Then came the
hordes of unchristianised peoples, who swooped
down upon the corrupt lands of Southern Europe
and Northern Africa.   They found a civilisation
which had become utterly corrupt, and which was
slowly paralysing the energies of the Church which
it had been compelled to recognise.   People who
inveigh against the Church for its apparent in-
activity during the next twelve or thirteen centuries
in a missionary direction should master the facts
of the case.   They should consider what it meant
to carry Christianity to every home in Europe;
and not to carry the mere message of a passing
missionary, but to introduce it as a working force,
gradually, painfully, into the family and social and
national life and consciousness.   They should con-

sider again that Christianity had to reckon with various enormous problems without whose solution the Church would remain unfitted to conquer the world. The great problems of theology had to be faced; the discussions of the theological centuries, down to the eighth century, and the remarkable discussions of the Reformation were absolutely necessary. There is much to say even for the Scholasticism of the Middle Ages. The intellectual life cannot be kept out of religion. There can be no strong religious life unless the intellect is put into it with as much energy as the heart and the will. The gospel has not descended in set phrases, like pet dogmas, out of heaven. It is the life of a person with a person through a person ; and these personal relations must be described, if they are to be apprehended, and if human faith and life are to be fed upon them. But to describe the mutual relations of these persons is to face the greatest problems which Philosophy can hope to deal with. And inasmuch as the ultimate mysteries had long been matters of discussion even in heathen Greece and Rome, and these discussions had given rise to many schools, the Christian facts had to be submitted to scrutiny from the point of view of the philosophies which made the intellectual atmosphere of the Greek world. Hence theories and counter-theories arose, and all the enormous literature, the great developments of heresy and orthodoxy, the passion, the fervour, the love and the hate, so well known to the students of European history, gathered around these attempted solutions or descriptions of ultimate mysteries and the substance of the gospel. Men saw the vast importance of disowning whatsoever seemed to interfere with the integrity of the gospel or to undermine the magnificent certitude of the Christian consciousness. No one who sees how necessary all this intellectual labour was, and the various developments of doctrine which it involved,—no one who appreciates the enormous difference between the clearness of statement and the fulness of intellectual equipment with which a modern missionary can go out to the heathen world, compared with what was possible to the earliest missionaries in Germany and Great Britain, will fail to see also that those long centuries wherein the Church confined its energies to the deepening of the Christian life intellectually and socially in Europe were necessary to the future spread of the gospel over the world. " All this was not simply a waste of force in wandering away from the right path and returning to it again. Rather every step of this long progress was needful to the result, and survives as a necessary element in it. And if humanity had not already gone through such experience, it would require still to go through it, or something like it."[1]

At the same time it should be said that during those long centuries when Christianity practically mastered Europe, it was not entirely forgotten that the world is concerned in the gospel message. The American world was, of course, unknown until

[1] Professor Edward Caird on "Christianity and the Historical Christ," *The New Review*, March 1897, p. 10.

the sixteenth century.   Mohammedanism had swept down over Northern Africa, had covered Syria and Asia Minor with its relentless hordes, and had shut the doors of approach to Africa and Asia against the Church of Christ.   And yet we read of various efforts made by the Roman Church to establish its version of the Christian faith in China, in India, and in Africa long before the times of the modern movement had dawned.   As soon as the Americas were discovered, the work of evangelisation began there.   The Roman Church persisted in its own way until South America became almost entirely Roman   Catholic.   The   early   Colonists   from England, who chose Virginia and Maryland, as well as those who went to Pennsylvania and New England, recognised from the beginning that as Christians they owed a great debt to the Indian aborigines who had become their neighbours.   The charter of the original Virginia Company, which had a number of remarkable men on its London Board of Directors, contains a statement of the hope that the work of colonisation " may, by the providence of God, hereafter tend to the glory of His divine majesty in propagating the Christian religion to such peoples as yet lived in darkness and miserable ignorance of the true knowledge and worship of God, and may in time bring the infidels of these parts to human civility and to a settled and just government." [1]

[1] *Vide Life of · Nicholas Ferrar* (Longmans), p. 51.   *Vide* also *The Missionary Year Book*, 1889 (Fleming H. Revell Co., New York), p. 17 ff.

Even the East India Company, which in the days of its enormous wealth and power, at the close of last and the beginning of this century, so bitterly opposed the missionary movement, began its history in quite another spirit. "The charter of 1698 actually enacted that the Company should provide ministers who were to apply themselves to learn the native languages of the country where they shall reside, the better to enable them to instruct the Gentoos (as they called the Indians at first).that shall be servants or slaves to the said Company in the Protestant religion." It seems that the Directors did on one or two occasions send Bibles in several languages, and Catechisms, in order to fulfil this provision in their charter.

The earlier Protestant attempts at missions were hampered by the fact that the Church was still almost universally under State patronage. Officialism has always tended to starve evangelisation of every kind. For evangelism lives on the free impulses of love, and officialism cannot live without the bonds of red tape, which curb individual impulse. It was not until communities arose like the Moravians, or the Churches of North America, that the conditions for permanent missionary effort were established. When free Churches were established in England, and when, through them, societies were formed for the specific object of carrying the gospel to the whole world, then in all its marvellousness the modern missionary movement arose. At last the conditions had been created which made it possible for the

Church intelligently, deliberately, and powerfully to plan for the evangelisation of all the nations of mankind. Freedom at last from State persecution ; freedom also from ecclesiastical politics; dependence upon, and organisation of, the direct interest, prayers, faith, and sacrifices of the individual members of the Christian Church—these were the conditions within the Church which it had taken nineteen centuries to attain, and which made at last the conquest of the world an intelligent aim.

A brief summary of the argument of this chapter would emphasise the following points. Religion has attained true universality in Christianity. This universality is seen alike in the truths which constitute its central teaching and in the spirit with which it fills its adherents. The truths are such as to awaken reverence and even love for man as man, to deepen our feeling of awe in view of the dignity of his nature and the greatness of his destiny. The spirit is seen in that wide beneficence and self-sacrifice which from the beginning characterised the Church of Christ, which has passed, it is true, through many phases, but has shone out in this century more radiant and far-reaching than at any previous period of its history.

Whether this universalism of Christianity is more than a theory of theologians or a dream of enthusiasts may be a matter of question. It is quite legitimate to ask if the alleged universalism is being realised by Christianity becoming the sole and universal religion of mankind. I hope in the following chapters to deal with that question, the intention being to obtain an idea of the extent of this movement, the methods in which the spirit of beneficence just alluded to has taken effect, and the results for the human race which have followed or are following its operations.

*

CHAPTER III

In the beginning of the century and up to about the year 1870 the missionary was popularly classed amongst the adventurers. A halo of romance encircled his name wherever his reports were read. When he returned to the homeland, his public addresses were made before large and enthusiastic crowds; his exhibits of curios from native lands were gazed upon with intense delight; his descriptions of the manners and customs obtaining in the sphere of his travels and labours were listened to with bated breath. Magazines did not exist then in the abundance which bewilders our minds to-day, and those which did exist had not learned the art of catering to the public taste for whatever is novel, foreign, and sensational. The missionary supplied that lack, and fascinated many whose minds were by no means deeply interested in the central meaning of his career.

And truly the missionary during the first decades of this great movement found himself a pioneer in almost every land whither he went.

Few Europeans, and in many cases none, had entered before him into the regions of his missionary service.   Travellers, like the great discoverer, Cook, in the South Seas, may have brought back records of islands discovered and brief descriptions of the inhabitants; but the missionary was to all intents and purposes the first man to attempt to establish a living and intelligent contact with these peoples.   Many of those travellers and traders who had preceded the missionary had failed to do anything to make their travels or their trade contribute to the real opening up of the countries which they visited. When Adoniram Judson went to Burmah, and Jones to Madagascar, and Williams to the South Seas, and Marsden to New Zealand, and Chalmers to New Guinea, and Mackay to Uganda, they found themselves, indeed, in lands and amongst peoples that had been in a sense already discovered; and yet they were in very truth pioneers. To them it was given to see much and to describe much which their transient predecessors had failed to notice or to make known.   The reports of these men, and of several hundreds like them, have proved to be of the utmost value in accumulating geographical information of every kind.   "Geography," it has been said, "is the most valuable of the allies of foreign missions, which have done in return, so much for the development and elevation of this most interesting and comprehensive of all the sciences." [1]

[1] Dr. George Smith, in *Missions at Home and Abroad*, p. 140.

The region of the world where missionaries have
done most as pioneers, or where their achievements
have been most striking and interesting, has undoubtedly been the "dark continent" of Africa.
It was in 1837 that Ludwig Krapf, a young student
from Basle, was sent out to Africa by the Church
Missionary Society. His efforts to settle in Abyssinia were in vain, and in 1844 he landed at Mom-
basa, one hundred and twenty miles north of
Zanzibar. He was joined by two men of like
spirit, Rebmann and Ehrhardt. In subsequent years
he made repeated journeys inland, penetrating far
into the heart of the continent, encountering many
dangers, both from wild beasts and savage peoples.
In 1856 the companions above named displayed
before the Royal Geographical Society in London
a map of the interior of Africa. It contained many
inaccuracies, no doubt, but its real discoveries were
so remarkable that the scientific world was
thoroughly stirred. From the impulse given by
these men, " Burton went forth—Speke and Grant
went forth." In the meantime there was living,
working and travelling in South Africa, a man
whose name was destined to a fame greater than
any of these explorers attained. David Livingstone
had already begun his series of great discoveries.
In 1849 he had reached Lake Ngami ; and had
become gradually convinced that north of the
regions which he had explored " the country beyond
was not the large sandy plateau of the philosophers."
His mind was made up to press on into those
unexplored territories in order to open them up

4

to missionary and other enterprises. Of his subsequent achievements this is no place to speak. His toils, his sufferings, his victories, are part of the heritage of every intelligent man and woman.[1]

The spirit of this man is abundantly revealed in the letters and the jottings in his journal towards the end of his life. With what courage he pressed on through all manner of difficulties, with what marvellous success he encountered and mollified the fierce opposition of the wildest tribes, remaining unarmed and never threatening to employ force, need not here be enlarged upon. When the first rumours that Livingstone was dead reached the homeland, the minds of many millions of people were aroused to the most intense interest in his career and achievements. The interest was deepened almost to a painful degree by the uncertainty which for long weeks filled many minds regarding the truth of these sad rumours. When at last, in 1874, the news was flashed over the land, that Livingstone's body had been carried hundreds of miles to the coast by two of his native servants, and that it was about to be brought to England in a ship of the Royal Navy, the excitement was universal. For a career like his, it seemed to be the only fitting earthly close, that his body should find its last resting-place among the illustrious dead in Westminster Abbey. The close of Livingstone's career was the opening of Africa to commerce and

[1] *Vide The Personal Life of David Livingstone*, by Professor Blaikie.

missions. Three or four of the leading missionary societies used the opportunity presented by the public enthusiasm to establish new missions in various parts of the vast regions now open to European influence. Commercial companies and individual traders of all kinds eagerly penetrated into these fields which promised such magnificent results to their enterprise.[1]

I wish to return to the thought that the chief work of missionaries, as pioneers, is not to be measured by the mere number of geographical and other discoveries which they have made. Their influence upon the world has mainly arisen from the fact that in nearly all parts of the world they have been the first Europeans who have really settled down and made their homes amongst heathen, and, oftentimes, amongst savage peoples. Their stations have thus naturally become well known as stages or places of call along the great trade routes, whether by land or by sea. The trader comes to think of the mission station as a place where life is more secure, and where gradually business becomes more abundant.[2] If it is true, on the one hand, that the instructions of the missionary gradually enlighten the people and make it less easy for an unscrupulous trader to cheat them right and left, it is true also, on the other hand, that the same instructions increase the appetite of the natives for the products of civilisation. Missionary work, as we shall see in a

---

[1] *L. M. C.*, vol. i. pp. 275 ff.

[2] Cf. the saving of Dr. Junker's life by Alex. Mackay, in *Mackay of Uganda*, pp. 315, 320.

later chapter, has always been found to stimulate
in every tribe or people the process of civilisation.
The mere pioneer trader has never succeeded in
doing so. His influence has not developed the
taste of the natives, has not made the places which
he visits more inviting for the occupancy of other
Europeans.   In West Africa, for example, the
extensive operations of traders, in connection with
the rubber trade, have the sole effect, even at this
day, of oppressing and degrading the natives.
Deliberate cruelty and persistent injustice may
gradually depopulate the country, but cannot
be said to open it up to any further connections
with the civilised world than are involved in the
mere processes of the one or two forms of trade
created by the natural products of the country.
The observations of missionaries and others in the
South Seas combine to corroborate this view that
the pioneer trader is unable to open up the lands
which he visits to a living and healthful connection
with the world at large.   The pioneer missionary,
on the other hand, as he remains in such a West
African village, which is suffering from the in-
cursions of the trader, sets forces agoing which
more or less speedily change the aspect of affairs.
He builds his house, opens his school, plans and
cultivates his garden, trains native servants to help
him, and advises the community at large regarding
their homes, clothing, tools, and gardens.   Thus a
demand is created for a larger trade in a higher
class of articles than had hitherto been supplied.
Shoddy stuffs, bead ornaments, and worthless

trinkets cease to attract purchasers. The village has fifty points of living interest in the world beyond its bounds for every one which it possessed before the missionary arrived. This aspect of the missionary's work deserves emphasis, because it is often supposed that the carrying of religion and trade to heathen lands are industries which have nothing in common. Some traders have even sought to describe missionary activity as an enemy of trade. As matter of fact, the worst kind of traders precede the missionary; the best kind almost always come after him.

It is worthy of record that it has in several instances been reserved for the medical missionary to open the way into countries which had strenuously resisted the approaches of civilised communities. Into Siam, Corea, and Cashmere, for example, scarce a ray of light from the Western world could find its way until the medical missionary daringly entered and touched the needs of men with his merciful hands. His power to help human beings in the hour of their greatest distress, and his persistent refusal to make any personal gain out of their gratitude, has over and over again broken down national prejudices and led to the emancipation of a people from the thraldom of its isolation. The magnificent courage of young Elmslie and his young wife in the conquest of Cashmere has written one of the most pathetic and brilliant pages of heroism and self-denial.

There is another direction in which missionaries have proved themselves of great service to mankind, namely, in the accumulation of scientific knowledge. Concerning this it is not within my purpose or plan to say much. But it may be of use to state a few of the leading facts. The missionary has proved himself a man of wider interests than some sections of society have attributed to him. From all parts of the world his contributions to science are numerous and valuable, and in some cases have proved themselves of first-class importance. If the "Transactions" of Botanical, Zoological, Geological, Archæological, Ethnological, Philological, and Geographical Societies in Germany, Britain, and America were ransacked, they would be found to contain well-nigh innumerable contributions, in the form of memoranda, reports, and discussions, which have been sent by missionaries from all over the world. The late Professor Agassiz said : "Few are aware how much we owe them (the missionaries), both for their intelligent observation of facts and for their collection of specimens. We must look to them not a little for aid in our efforts to advance future science."[1] A work known as *The Ely Volume* has been published in America, which confines itself almost entirely to the contributions made to science by the representatives of that great society, The American Board of Commissioners for Foreign Missions. Although thus restricted in its range, it amounts to a volume of over five hundred pages of small print, describing original discussions and observations in almost every department of science.

Among individual instances of service rendered

[1] Quoted in *The Ely Volume*, p. 122.

to science, two or three of the more remarkable examples may be given. Carey, the great missionary to India, who in the one task of mastering Oriental languages and translating the Scriptures may be said to have done the work of ten men, carried on at the same time most valuable investigations in a quite different direction. He was a keen observer of nature, and his love of botany led him to establish a large garden for the study of the Indian flora. His contributions to science concerning the natural history and botany of India were of such importance that he was elected to the Asiatic Society. But greater than that was the fact that he proposed and founded the Agricultural and Horticultural Society of India. At its first meeting only five were present. But so diligent and wise was he that it grew rapidly, and has exercised great influence in science and on the development of India.[1] In the South Seas there have lived and worked two brothers, Rev. J. T. Gulick and the Rev. L. Halsey Gulick, each of whom has done scientific work of unusual value. The former is the man whose name has been made so famous in recent days by its association with the development of thought through which the late George J. Romanes passed. He gave his attention to certain conditions of life obtaining in the Sandwich Islands, which seemed to him to illustrate the laws of the modification of species. The results of his observation and thought were

[1] *Vide* Dr. George Smith's splendid chapter, in his *Life of William Carey*, on "What Carey did for Science."

sent to the Linnæan Society in London. Concerning these communications, Mr. Romanes published the following opinion in the well-known weekly paper called *Nature* : [1]—" I cannot allow the present communication to appear in these columns without again recording my conviction that the writer is the most profound of living thinkers upon Darwinian topics, and that the generalisations which have been reached by his twenty years of thought are of more importance to the theory of evolution than any that have been published during the post-Darwinian period." We are told that the Rev. L. Halsey Gulick, while in Micronesia, made observations of a geographical and meteorological nature which are used to this day as a basis for drawing up charts of navigation.[2]

I have already adverted to the almost incalculable debt which geographical science owes to the travels and observations of missionaries in every part of the world. Carl Ritter, the most painstaking and influential of modern geographers, freely recognised the missionaries as indispensable coadjutors of his work. Of the *Missionary Herald* he says: " It is the repository to which the reader must look to find the most valuable documents that have ever been sent over by any society, and where a rich

---

[1] *Vide Nature*, April 10, 1890. The facts concerning Mr. Gulick's correspondence with Mr. Romanes are given in *Bibliotheca Sacra*, vol. liii. pp. 68, 69, and 165–167. In the same volume, Mr. Gulick's "Statement," made on the request of Mr. Romanes, entitled "Christianity and the Evolution of Rational Life," is printed in full, pp. 70–74. Cf. Romanes' *Thoughts on Religion*, *passim*.

[2] *Life*, by Frances Gulick Jewett, pp. 161 ff.

store of scientific, historical, and antiquarian details may be seen."[1] The same remark will apply in great measure to the organs of all the leading missionary societies.

It is, of course, in the region of anthropological science that the largest mass of materials has been contributed by the missionaries. They, it is safe to say, have become more intimately acquainted with the customs, institutions, not to speak of languages and religions,[2] of heathen peoples, than any other class of men. Allusion has been made to the many contributions sent by missionaries to the "Transactions" of learned societies and to the pages of missionary magazines. The scientific value of these is of course far surpassed by the volumes of all kinds, large and small, learned and popular, which missionaries have written during this century. They will be found to deal in varying degrees of fulness and detail with the history, religion, language, physical conditions, government and social life of most of the peoples of heathendom. No one who has not glanced over a large missionary library, *and discovered how incomplete it is*, can have any conception of the extent of this literature. And no one who has not read pretty widely in it can have any idea of its value in relation to the subjects above named.

The missionary may then be looked upon, in the light of what has been said of his influence as a

---

[1] Professor G. Frederick Wright, D.D., in *Missions at Home and Abroad*, p. 351.

[2] *Vide* p. 173, note.

traveller and a recorder of facts, as a considerable force in the development of the race during this century. But there is one point regarding his function in this development which is of peculiar significance. If the facts stated above, and those which I hope to establish in the following chapters, are facts, and are correctly interpreted, it follows that the missionary movement has done more than anything else to hasten the reunion of the race. The unity of mankind may or may not have been a realised fact in the beginning of history; but since the time when seas and mountains, deserts and rivers, first broke the race up into isolated and independent sections, that unity has been more of an ideal or a dream than a living and concrete truth. The nations have been divided from one another for many ages; there has been little or no interchange of intellectual, religious, or social influence. Even the extension of the Roman Empire over many races did not, and could not, serve to make them one in more than a merely formal sense. In all that made life what it was to each of them, they were separated from one another. To-day we are in presence of a most remarkable phenomenon. The basis is being laid deep in the consciousness of every people on earth which makes it possible for all peoples to realise their common brotherhood, and to feel the fascination of a reunited humanity. The force which more than any other is working towards this consummation is the Christian religion. Deep down below those levels of thought and emotion which are touched by commerce, war, politics, industry, or secular education, it is doing this work. It is the religious impulse which alone accounts for the career of the missionary. He becomes the pioneer who makes his home far in advance of all other Europeans within the confines of heathendom and savagery, because he has heard what he names "the call of God," and has felt the mysterious impulse which he and all who think with him attribute to the Spirit of Jesus Christ. It is only the communication of this religious experience to heathen men and women which is creating the conditions for that unity of sentiment and life towards which the world is moving. For when the missionary has succeeded in winning converts, the latter receive a new consciousness regarding their relations to the world at large. As we shall see in greater detail, and be compelled to emphasise again, it is out of this community of religious experience that the other affiliations of race with race and tribe with tribe are developing before the eyes of us all. If the work were not proceeding so quietly and steadily, if its most important operations were not being carried on in the deeper regions of religious attainment and moral development, and if its sphere were not so vast, comprehending all nations and languages, more of us would be astounded by the thing which is happening in our generation. Humanity is becoming one organism. But the life which is permeating the separate members, many of which were almost fatally atrophied, is the life of the Christian

religion.   And this life is at present working
through the class of men whom we call missionaries.
Throughout the world in their myriads of mission
stations, on lonely islands, and amongst teeming
Oriental cities, they are all ceaselessly busied about
their magnificent task.   The army seems scattered,
but it is thoroughly organised, and it is the most
effective instrument ever dreamed of by men for
making one humanity out of the scattered and
isolated tribes of earth.   The missionaries are all
drawing the hearts of mankind to one centre of
supreme interest and infinite power.   Ask them
all in their scattered stations, lonely and yet not
alone, what motive has brought them there, and
why there is this extraordinary identity of aim and
of influence pervading all their separate spheres
of labour, and they unanimously give one name as
the explanation of these facts.   It is the name of
Jesus Christ.

CHAPTER IV

ONE of the most remarkable and impressive phases of the history of the Christian Church is undoubtedly the circulation of the Bible throughout the world, as that has been achieved during this century. I propose in this chapter to describe briefly the extent, the cost, and the effects of that work.

At the end of last century the Scriptures had been translated into less than fifty languages. That number was of course, in large measure, confined to the languages of Europe. As soon as the movement outwards to the great world of heathendom began, attention was directed to the necessity for giving the Bible, in their own languages, to those who were to be evangelised. It is well known how early the founders of missions in the East directed, and how completely some of them concentrated, their attention upon this task. William Carey and Henry Martyn in India, deeply as they longed and hard as they laboured for the conversion of individuals to the Christian faith, yet

allowed nothing to interfere with their pursuit of
the ideal which glowed before their minds, that,
namely, of giving to the peoples of India the Word
of God in their own tongues. Indeed, of Martyn
it is said that " His devotion to the study of the
languages which interpret and apply to the races
of India, Asia, and Persia, the books of the Christian revelation, was so absorbing as to shorten
his career." [1]

It was not long before the friends of the gospel
in the homelands found that this work must be
undertaken by special agencies, and that the
ordinary missionary societies could not grapple
with the task of superintending the printing and
publishing of the Scriptures. Hence arose the
Bible Societies. These institutions, which now
number nearly one hundred all over Christendom,
comprise many whose work is almost purely local,
and is confined to the dissemination of the Scriptures. The larger and graver task has devolved
almost exclusively upon five or six societies. Of
these the best known are the British and Foreign
Bible Society, the American Bible Society, and
the National Bible Society of Scotland.

Concerning the largest Bible Societies two facts
of delightful significance ought to be recorded. In
the first place, they have co-operated with great
magnanimity and unfailing courtesy with all kinds
of missionary societies. Their connections with
some of the societies have been peculiarly intimate
and constant. Negotiations regarding the making

---

[1] *Life of Henry Martyn*, by Dr. George Smith, p. 419.

and printing of translations, regarding the payment of missionaries as translators, revisers, proof-readers, etc., and regarding the supply of Bibles and portions to the various fields where they were needed, and payment for the same, have often involved delicate personal and other matters. But the whole spirit of their ideal has entered into the hearts and minds of these directors and informed their dealings with one another. In the second place, the Bible Societies have offered to the world the spectacle of at least one platform on which all who are of evangelical faith can stand together. The British and Foreign and the American Bible Societies both describe the aim of their existence in identical terms: "its sole object shall be to encourage a wide circulation of the Holy Scriptures without note or comment." They are almost the only institutions of an interdenominational character which have survived the tendency to form denominational societies.

An idea of the amount of energy and devotion which is annually spent on this work may be gathered from a glance at the figures which these societies published for the year 1895. In that year the British and Foreign Bible Society had an income of £213,962, and circulated 3,970,439 copies of Bibles, New Testaments, and portions of the Bible. The American Bible Society had an income of £87,444, and circulated 1,750,283 copies. The National Bible Society of Scotland had an income of £28,976, and circulated 814,408 copies. The three societies together had an income

of £330,380 and circulated 6,535,130 copies. It
has been computed that the thirty largest Bible
Societies had up to the year 1893 put into circulation no fewer than 250,000,000 copies of either the
whole Bible or a portion of it. This vast amount
of work is being carried on day by day by means
of the ordinary missionary agencies, and by
means also, in many lands, of colporteurs appointed
and supported by the respective Bible Societies,
for the express work of distributing or selling
the Scriptures and explaining their teaching
whenever they can find opportunity. The latter
are among the most efficient agencies at present
working for the redemption of the world. They
must be men of great devotion, of constant and
ready wit, able to suit themselves to each emergency,
and to have an answer at once wise and attractive
for all the abundant words of opposition or ridicule
which are cast upon the book which they sell and
the work of selling it which they have undertaken.
High among those who have done great things for
the Kingdom of God will stand the name of many
a colporteur whose fame has not gone far in the
world.

It requires a considerable effort of the imagination to realise the extent of the work, and still
more the extent of its influence, as the task of
Bible distribution proceeds throughout the world.
Let me state a few facts bearing upon various
aspects of the work in various parts of the world
to aid our imagination. The Bible, which, as I
have said, existed in less than fifty translations at

the end of last century, has now been translated, and is now published, in whole or part, in nearly four hundred languages and dialects. So persistent and serious has been the toil of missionaries over this one great task that in a recent period of ten years (1882-1892) no fewer than fifty new translations were made. There are many native languages in Africa into which no translation has yet been possible. There are probably districts in India and China in a similar position. There are probably some more important languages in Central Asia to which this supreme evidence of admission to a central place in the world's history has not yet come. But nine-tenths of the peoples of the world speak the languages into which translations have been made, while only one-tenth speak the tongues as yet unconquered for this end. It is true, therefore, to say, that now at last no considerable section of the world's inhabitants speaking one language is without the Scriptures.

A few facts illustrative of details may help us to realise the character and extent of the work. The National Bible Society of Scotland has divided China into five great agencies. In them it employs eight European agents, and one hundred and fifty native colporteurs. The work of these men is to go from place to place striving to get the people to buy the Scriptures. They speak to them, explain the nature of the strange wares which they offer, answer difficult questions, read passages in order to whet the appetite and excite the curiosity. But they neither preach nor teach in any stated place.

5

Their life work is to scatter the Scriptures. This army, representing only one Society, did in China in 1896 dispose of 379 Bibles, 5246 Testaments and 208,165 portions, making a total of 213,790 copies of Scripture sold. Turn to another religion. In the Turkish Empire two books compete for supremacy over the religious life of its inhabitants, viz., the Koran and the Bible. Now, the Mohammedan religion forbids that its sacred books be translated out of the holy Arabic language into infidel tongues; and any Turkish subject who is found with a copy of such translation has to forfeit it that it may be committed to the flames. But the Christian Bible is now translated into eleven of the languages spoken within the boundaries of that empire, and no fewer than fifty or sixty thousand copies are sold annually.

The story of the labour involved in the translation of the Bible into more than three hundred languages, and its revision in many cases over and over again, can probably never be fully told. It lies buried in the records of the various missionary societies. Nay, much of it is not even there. For missionaries, as a class, do not complain of their toil nor recount its details. Their periodical reports seldom reflect with any adequacy the weariness, the monotony, or, at times, the drudgery of their daily life. Hence the difficulties which have been encountered and surmounted must be largely left to our imagination, working upon certain general facts and multiplying these into the effort and the silent endurance of months and years and decades.

The great work of Bible translation and distribution is going on everywhere continually. The labourers are well-nigh innumerable, their toil incalculable. None of them is paid in cash according to the commercial value of his work. They all do this work out of the depths of a passionate love. They may be utterly wrong, their love indefensible, their toil a stupendous blunder. But there it is, stupendous at any rate, and covering the earth more and more completely year by year. These untiring toilers are placing in more and more homes among all peoples, without any discrimination whatsoever, the pages of this unique book, the silent witness of the origin of the Christian man's faith and the grounds of his eternal hope.

The difficulties have varied, of course, in kind and degree according to circumstances. Sometimes the work of translation has been undertaken by men of comparatively high scholarship, men who, like Henry Martyn, enjoyed the advantages of a thorough university education. At other times it has been entered upon by men like William Carey, who, without a thorough preparation, yet possessed a native genius for the acquisition of languages. But in a large number, perhaps in the majority of cases, the labour of translation has been undertaken by men who neither had a high training nor natural genius for linguistic work. They were men of good natural ability, who never would have entered upon any such effort in their homelands, but who, having given themselves to the task of converting heathen into Christian peoples, and finding a translated Bible quite essential, set themselves with a stubbornness born of their central aim and deepest passion to the mastery of a native language, and oftentimes to the acquisition or deeper study of Hebrew and Greek. For example, can anything be more pathetic than the position of the first missionaries to Greenland, who found themselves unable to reach the people without the Scriptures, and yet unable to translate them, because they were uneducated men, without a knowledge of the grammar of their own language! Yet these men did surmount even these frowning mountains of difficulty by the exercise of a humble and patient courage, and began to reduce the Esquimaux language to writing. They and their successors toiled at the work till the entire Scriptures were translated. Or even consider the case of a man like Robert Moffat. He went out to South Africa with only the most meagre and hurried education. He was a man first and last of outward activity, who made *con amore* long journeys, planted and cultivated large and beautiful gardens, loved, in fact, the open air and physical activity. Yet that man persisted for many years in the task of translation, studied various versions of the Scriptures, spent hours, and even days, over one verse or clause, to find the exact shade of meaning and put it into an equivalent native idiom. The result was that he performed the rare task of translating the whole Bible with his own hand, completing the New Testament in 1838 and the entire book in 1857.

Yet again, the difficulties which have been over-come must be estimated by a glance at the variety of languages into which these translations have been made. In some cases, those, for example, of Chinese, Hindustani, Sanskrit, Persian, etc., missionaries found a more or less elaborate native literature. For centuries, literary idioms and fashions had been formed and very extensive vocabularies developed. The man who desired to see the Scriptures take rank at once at the head of an already abundant native literature must master those vocabularies, and whether he employ them all or not, he must be familiar enough with the idioms and literary forms, that he may choose which would best suit the varied portions of the Scriptures. Henry Martyn was wisely advised by a well-known Orientalist of his day not to begin translating till he had "resided some years in the country. He said it was the rock on which mission-aries had split, that they had attempted to write and preach before they knew the language. The Lord's Prayer was now a common subject of ridicule with the people, on account of the manner in which it had been translated."[1] William Carey, in many ways the greatest missionary of them all, found himself under necessity to master Sanskrit, which he calls "perhaps the hardest language in the world"; but he set himself to it with his invincible powers of application. So early as 1798 he says: "I have nearly translated the Sanskrit grammar and dictionary into English, and have

[1] *Life*, by Dr. Geo. Smith, p. 72.

made considerable progress in compiling a dictionary, Sanskrit, including Bengali and English."
Even in the case of these literary languages the
difficulties were not confined to the mastery of
idioms and finding of appropriate translations.
Referring to his earliest Bengali version in 1800,
he says: "In the printing I have to look over
the copy and correct the press, which is much
more laborious than it would be in English, because
spelling, writing, printing, etc., in Bengali is almost
a new thing, and we have in a manner to fix the
orthography."[1]   In spite of these difficulties, which
presented themselves in connection with each language which Carey and his colleagues undertook
to learn and to use for translation purposes, he
succeeded in either translating, or superintending
the translation of, the Bible in whole or part into
no fewer than thirty-six languages.   The whole
Scriptures had been at the time of his death, 1834,
translated into seven languages (Bengali, Orissa,
Assamese, Sanskrit, Hindi, Marathi, and Chinese).
"The Bengali, Hindi, Marathi, and Sanskrit
translations were his own.   The Chinese was
similarly the work of Marshman (his colleague).
The Hindi versions in their many dialects, and
the Orissa, were blocked out by his colleagues
and the pundits.   He saw through the press
the Hindustani, Persian, Malay, Tamil, and
other versions of the whole or portions of the
Scriptures.   He ceased not night and day, if by
any means, with a loving catholicity, the Word of

---

[1] *Life*, by Dr. George Smith, 2nd ed., p. 188.

God might be given to the millions."[1] The life-work of William Carey is one of the most wonderful which our world has seen, not less for its difficulty, its amount, its enthusiasm, and its influence on the history of the race, than for the humility, the gentleness, the patience of the great heart that undertook and carried it forward without weariness until the close of his arduous and brilliant career.

When we turn to the unwritten languages of the simpler peoples, we find the missionary facing problems of another but oftentimes no less puzzling kind. The learning of the language must be derived wholly from conversation, and the grammar mastered very slowly and painfully, as the inflections and constructions grow familiar. Then follows the task of finding letters to represent the various sounds. When these difficulties have been surmounted, the preacher and translator finds himself in many cases confronted by the fact that the natives, having very poor ideas of a spiritual world, have no words to express the central facts contained in the message of the gospel. It is only with extreme labour, care, and patience that words are gradually found which can be used without misunderstanding or with a minimum of danger. Then these words have to be explained with new shades of meaning, so that a gradual transformation is effected, such as took place in many Greek words when they came to be used for the purposes of Christian experience and Christian

[1] *Life*, by Dr. George Smith, p. 214.

thought at the beginning of our era. No one who
has not attempted this task, or heard much about
it and pondered it sympathetically, can easily
conceive of the work which it has implied and
implies to-day throughout the world. Some cases
of difficulty have occasioned considerable con-
troversy, as in China, where there has been serious
difference of opinion regarding the word which
should be employed for the name of God. In a
certain part of India difficulty has been found with
the word "flesh." The nearest native equivalent
which could be found meant "flesh-meat" in
distinction from bone or blood. It is easy to see
what ludicrous misunderstandings this word would
suggest in many parts of Scripture. For example,
one native, on the text, "I will not fear what flesh
can do unto me," said: "It is plain enough, but it
is a very curious thing to say. It means of course,
'I will not fear even though the eating of flesh
causes me indigestion.'" In Japanese the translators, finding no word for "kiss," had to manu-
facture one, and then, I suppose, had to explain its
meaning. In a certain West African language,
the missionaries found that in translating the
word "heaven," they had employed a native word
signifying only "at the top of a tree" or "of a
pole." But nowhere has there been serious failure
of perseverance and faithfulness. Everywhere
these and many other difficulties have been or are
being gradually overcome, and the natives are receiving in their own language this book of God.

Thus far I have attempted to describe the

extent and nature of this work of translating the Bible which has proceeded at so rapid a rate during this century of foreign missions. Let me now attempt to describe something of the value of this kind of labour to the Church and to mankind at large. It may be assumed that there must be some deep significance attaching to this volume which has made it seem not only worth while, but morally imperative, to so many men in so many parts of the world to engage in its translation.

First of all, it is obvious that, judged even from the scientific point of view, these achievements must have a great value. One of the many fields in which our century has seen scientific advance of an almost incalculable extent is that of language. Comparative Philology and Comparative Grammar are children of only a recent generation, and yet no one man is now able to follow out all their ramifications for himself at first hand. The languages of all races are being subjected to the closest scrutiny, and the results are being used to throw light upon other most important departments of investigation. For example, Ethnology, while it owes much to the study of the anatomy of the races, especially to craniology, and much also to archæology, with its investigation of the relics of antiquity and comparison of these with utensils and weapons in use to-day, yet derives a large mass of its material, sometimes the most certain and trustworthy, from the labours which have been spent upon the comparative study of languages. The same is true of the science of Com-

parative Religion.   Professor Max Müller has made
us familiar with some of the invaluable results
which accrue to that science from a careful study
of the history of significant words.   Now it is
perfectly safe to say, that no one body of men has
done so much to make the widest and most thorough
study of languages possible as the missionaries of
the nineteenth century.   This is a glory, which,
like the glory of the pioneer and observer of natural
life, can only belong in a much less degree to the
men who go out into the field in the next or any
later century.   Through all history, the nineteenth
century will be remembered for this.   Many of its
other scientific attainments will be surpassed and
remembered only by the most minute student of
the history of physics and biology.   But no student
of language will ever be able to forget that it was
in the nineteenth century that all the principal
languages of the world were used for the translation of this one book, and thus a universal basis of
linguistic comparison was established.   In that
future time many languages and dialects will have
disappeared, of which no record would or could
have been kept other than these translations of
Scripture which have been made by missionaries
of our own and three preceding generations.
Professor Max Müller has emphasised the importance of missionaries in elucidating the problems of
the dialectic life of language.   He says that
"whatever is known of the dialects of savage
tribes is chiefly or entirely due to the missionary."[1]

[1] Max Müller's *Science of Language*, vol. i., pp. 58, 471.

It is easy to see many reasons why this should be the case. Not only are missionaries in the very large majority of cases the only Europeans or Americans of education who make prolonged residence among savage peoples, and so have fullest opportunities for mastery of native languages; they are also bound by the most solemn motives of their lives to give the closest attention to the study of these languages. They know that with imperfect idioms and inaccurate pronunciation, they seriously hamper their work; while the more completely they speak as the natives do, the more deep and persuasive is the spiritual influence which they may hope to exert. Hence we have the spectacle of literally thousands of men and women all over the world, who have obtained a familiarity with many scores of languages, such as few scholars would or could have attained, in the mere interests of philological research. Moreover, these missionaries have done more than merely translate the Scriptures. In nearly all cases it has been found necessary, in order to teach the natives, to write and publish lesson-books, grammars, and in very many cases even dictionaries of the native languages. Some of these works have proved to be of immense importance to scholarship in the most important Oriental languages. For example, there is the great Chinese dictionary of Robert Morrison, in six large quarto volumes, which he compiled through sixteen years of incessant labour, and which cost the East India Company over ten thousand pounds to print.

This work had compelled Morrison to gather a library of ten thousand Chinese books, and it contained fifty thousand words printed in Chinese characters. It has been the basis of all future progress in the scientific study of that language.

The breadth of view, the calm and yet strong powers of discrimination which have been displayed by many of these men, find nowhere more adequate expression than in a letter of Carey's, written in 1811. "I have of late been much impressed with the vast importance of laying a foundation for Biblical criticism in the East by preparing grammars of the different languages into which we have translated or may translate the Bible. Without some such step, they who follow us will have to wade through the same labours that I have, in order to stand merely upon the same ground that I now stand upon. If, however, elementary books are provided, the labour will be greatly contracted; and a person will be able in a short time to acquire that which has cost me years of study and toil. The necessity which lies upon me of acquiring so many languages, obliges me to study and work out the grammars of each of them, and to attend closely to their irregularities and peculiarities. I have, therefore, already published grammars of three of them, viz., the Bengali, the Sanskrit, and the Mahratta. To these I have resolved to add the grammars of the Telinga, Kurnata, Orissa, Punjabi, Kashmeeri, Gujarati, Nepalese, and Assam languages. Two of these are now in the press, and I hope to have two or three more of them out by the last of next year." "These," he adds, with quiet humour, "may not only be useful in the way I stated, but may serve to furnish an answer to a question which has more than once been repeated: 'How can these men translate in so great a number of languages?' Few people know what may be done till they try, and persevere in what they undertake."[1] In the library of Serampore College there are preserved five colossal volumes of a polyglot dictionary which had been prepared by the Carey band of workers for use in the translation of the Bible.

Surely no higher service can be rendered to a people than that which Dante did for Italy, and Luther for Germany, and the translators of the English Bible for the English-speaking race, when to these lands and races books were given which once for all made each of these languages a literary vehicle, and through it gradually penetrated the great masses of the people with the glory of new and inspiring ideas. Yet this has been done over and over again in our own day for various peoples by these missionaries of the Christian religion. This thought has been finely expressed by Dr. George Smith in his *Life of William Carey*.[2] "Like the growth of a tree is the development of a language, as really and as strictly according to law. In savage lands like those of Africa, the

[1] *Life*, by Dr. George Smith, pp. 220, 221.
[2] Pp. 241 f.

missionary finds the living germs of speech, arranges them for the first time in grammatical order, expresses them in written and printed form, using the simplest and most perfect and most universal character of all—the Roman, and at one bound gives the most degraded of the dark peoples the possibility of the highest civilisation and the divinest future. In countries like India and China, where civilisation has long ago reached its highest level, and has been declining for want of the salt of a universal Christianity, it is the missionary again who interferes for the highest ends, but by a different process. Mastering the complex classical speech and literature of the learned and priestly class, and living with his Master's sympathy among the people whom that class oppresses, he takes the popular dialects which are instinct with the life of the future; where they are widely luxuriant he brings them under law, where they are barren he enriches them from the parent stock, so as to make them the vehicles of ideas such as the Greek gave to Europe, and in time he brings to the birth nations worthy of the name by a national language and literature lighted up with the ideas of the book which he is the first to translate. This was what Carey did for the speech of the Bengalees."

It is only necessary to do here, as we must in the other studies of missionary labour in which we engage, exert our imagination to see this kind of work being done in varying measure throughout the world. Wherever these more than three hundred and fifty languages and dialects are spoken, the missionary is at work translating the Bible verse by verse, writing the lesson-books, the grammars, the vocabularies and dictionaries, the hymn-books, the prayer-books, the evangelistic tracts, and the school geographies, histories, and so on. Then we may grasp, but even then only faintly, the enormous service to the science of language which has been rendered by the spread of Christian missions.

It is time now to approach this matter from a more intimate point, from that, namely, of the Christian religion itself. It is a natural question to ask: Why has all this labour been undertaken? It is obvious that no mere scientific interest could possibly have led to such self-denial. No man ever thought of translating the Bible into a barbarian tongue, for the sake of philology. Many great Oriental scholars have been interested in the languages of India and China and their literatures, but very few of them have cared much about the provision of a higher or better literature for the people who speak those languages. It is the religious motive alone which can account for this work. To the Christian man one of the most solemn and indisputable obligations of life is, to seek the salvation of the world. His loyalty to Jesus Christ includes loyalty to the sublime purpose of Christ. His acceptance of that which he believes and feels to be the supreme grace of God, makes him a debtor to the world. He is recreant to the noblest instincts of the new heart and the new life, if he cherishes no desire and makes no effort to see this divine experience pass to other men and women. Hence the willingness of hundreds of missionaries to undertake the kind of work which we have been trying to measure and understand. For the Bible is deemed essential by all evangelical Christians to a healthful Christian life. The Mohammedan may be able to count up his converts in Central Africa by hundreds when they have only the most meagre conception of the teaching of the Koran. The Roman Catholic may be content to count as converts to Christianity all those whom he can persuade to be baptised, to learn certain prayers and attend the mass. But the evangelical Christian has at once a harder and a higher task before him. He will not baptise until he has somewhat adequately taught his catechumen; and he does not consider that teaching is sufficient until the Spirit of God has given evident signs of His will in the matter, by a changed mind and heart, and a transformed manner of life.

Now this teaching, which is absolutely essential, cannot be carried on by mere word of mouth, by committing to memory the sayings and traditions on which faith fastens, and by which conduct is moulded. The hope of the Christian religion lies in the constant presentation of its substance to the minds of men through the Scriptures. For it is a clear lesson of past experience, that wheresoever this ceases to be done, the power of this religion begins to wane, and the outlines of a Christian character begin to grow dim. The effect of Christianity upon the social and family and individual life of the European peoples has always been proportionate to their familiarity with the person and the work of the Saviour as He is depicted in the New Testament. In those countries where the Bible has been a sealed book, the priest has stepped forth to occupy its place, and has striven to become the medium of communication between the human spirit and the divine. That has always meant a more or less rapid descent into ignorance, superstition, and practical heathenism. As soon as the Bible has broken through the fetters of priestcraft, and once more found admittance to the homes of the people, the life of direct fellowship with God has been once more established. The most striking proofs of the effect of the Bible are to be found in the contrast between Roman Catholic missions, with their results in heathen lands, and Evangelical missions. It is well known that India and Japan were mission fields of the Church of Rome centuries before the Protestant world thoroughly awoke to its task. It is also well known that these missions, apparently successful as far as number was concerned, did almost nothing to illumine and purify the peoples. They substituted new idols, as it seemed, for the old; new priesthoods for the old; new forms and more solemn rites of worship. But still baptism and the mass simply took the place of the other magic acts to which supernatural efficacy had already been attributed. No Bible meant practically no Christ, and no Christ meant no living

6

faith, no consciousness of fellowship with God.[1]
But where that is not attained, Christianity is not
attained, the real heart of the religion and its most
sublime boon is not realised.

What, then, has been the result in this one
regard of the wide-extended translation of the
Scriptures during this century? In a word, it
may be said that abundant testimony comes from
all the regions where these four hundred modern
versions are being circulated, and the testimony
combines to show that it is beyond human language
to express the influence of this unique volume.
Many, of course, have read it and have not become
Christians. But this is only what the nature of
the religion and its history from the beginning,
aye, from the hour when they shouted, "Crucify
Him," would lead us to expect. The significant
facts are connected with the multitudes who,
through the reading of these pages, have found
coming upon them the same experience as upon
all who have entered into the true Christian life,
from the time of the apostles to our own. The
fact is, that the preaching and teaching missionaries
are in some lands outstripped by this silent herald
of divine truth. We are told that the very first
edition of Carey's translation of the New Testament
into Bengali, imperfect as it was, was not without
its self-evidencing power   "Seventeen years after,
when the mission extended to the old capital of

[1] It is a remarkable fact that the successors of St. Francis
Xavier in Japan translated a good many books, and tried to
educate the people, but the Bible was not translated.

Dacca, there were found several villages of Hindu-
born peasants who had given up idol-worship, were
renowned for their truthfulness, and, as searching
for a true teacher come from God, called themselves
'Satya-gooroos.' They traced their new faith to
a much-worn book kept in a wooden box in one
of their villages.   No one could say whence it had
come; all they knew was that they had possessed
it for many years.   It was Carey's first Bengali
version of the New Testament of our Lord and
Saviour Jesus Christ.   In the wide and elastic
bounds of Hinduism, and even amid fanatical
Mussulmans beyond the frontier, the Bible, dimly
understood without a teacher, has led to puritan
sects like this."[1]

Or take an instance from another land.   In
Japan there arose a few years ago a young man,
Neesima, who did more for the higher education
of his fellow-countrymen than any other.   He was
the far-sighted and enthusiastic founder of the
Doshisha, the pioneer university, if we may use
the term, among that remarkable and fascinating
people.   Neesima was a man of remarkable Christian
experience, who throughout his educational labours
kept in view the evangelisation of his country.   He
was born and brought up in a family where he had
no opportunity to learn aught of the Christian
religion.   At about twenty years of age he stumbled
on a book in Chinese which consisted of extracts
from the Bible.   These broken pieces of the story
of revelation awoke him.   He determined to dis-

[1] *Life of William Carey*, by Dr. George Smith.

cover more about this marvellous, this illuminating literature. It was during that dark period when Japan was closed to foreigners, and Neesima, seeing no hope of light unless from foreigners, fled his country. He reached Singapore, and there, finding a copy of the Scriptures for sale, he actually, and against the whole sentiment and tradition of his class, sold his sword in order to purchase this book. Hearing that from America the men had come who knew most about this book, he resolved to sail thither. On the voyage he read alone and unaided in its pages. At last those words which have proved themselves light and life to so many of the sons of men passed under his scrutiny : " God so loved the world that He gave His only begotten Son, that whosoever believeth on Him should not perish, but have everlasting life." This verse was his golden gate, and Neesima was one more added to the innumerable host who, through the central message of this book, have found a living and personal fellowship with the living God.

Or, again, take the case of Madagascar, during the great persecution which lasted nearly a quarter of a century. The missionaries, after barely twenty years of work in that country, were compelled to leave. They left nothing behind them except the Bible, and the men and women who had already become Christians. But that was enough. When the enemy came, and the churches were broken up, this book was multiplied enormously in value. Copies of it were most carefully hidden away. People would walk long distances to have it read in secret or to buy even a very small portion of it. Those who could read taught others, and the message with its strange power was spreading even through flames and torture and bloodshed. The result was, that when the country was opened again to civilisation, the missionaries, who were of course the first to enter, found that, although thousands of Christians had been put to death, there were more Christians at the end of the long trial than at the beginning. Undoubtedly this most remarkable outcome of that protracted and systematic effort to exterminate the Christian Church was due almost entirely to the fact that the Bible had been translated and circulated, and could be read at first hand. Mere preaching could not have done it; organisation had nothing to do with it. It was the Scriptures, possessed and owned by the people, which maintained and increased their enthusiasm for the faith and life of the Christian Church.

Or, again, let us pass into Central Africa, up into the great kingdom of Uganda where Mackay laboured, and where the brave Bishop Hannington perished. No story of missions during the last quarter of a century is more inspiring, more thrilling, almost overawing, than the story of Uganda. Here again we find that from the very first the missionaries aimed at translating and circulating the Scriptures. The consequence is seen to-day in the intense interest of those people, so recently savage, in every sense of the term, in this book. They buy it as fast as it can be supplied. They read it in their homes, discuss its histories, its teachings, in twos and threes, in families and casual groups. They borrow English reference Bibles from the missionaries to aid them in their study. To them, as to the hunted martyrs of Madagascar, as to the learned pundits and deeply religious peasants of India, as to the enthusiastic youth of Japan, this book has brought light and purity, the awakening of mind and heart to the noblest ideals and highest hopes.

Go throughout the world, and the result is the same. In Bolivia, a colporteur, entering a mere hovel of the poorest description, finds a man reading a book which he hurriedly tries to hide. It is the Spanish Protestant Bible. Inquiry proves that he thoroughly enjoys it, and that more than twenty of his companions are reading the same copy. In Italy, where Romanism has done her best to keep this book from the people, it can be kept no longer. Educated people, whether passionately sceptical or Romanist, are one after another conquered by it. An army officer sternly prohibits the sale of the book amongst his soldiers. One of his own attendants secretly buys a copy, which the officer begins to read. It conquers him, and he becomes a man of the book. These are mere specimens brought from here and there among various classes and races of men. They are bits of evidence which we must multiply by thousands and tens of thousands, if we would give them their scientific value. The two hundred and fifty millions of copies of the Bible, circulated in four hundred versions throughout the world, are doing this kind of work throughout all nations. The educated and the savage, the hardened cannibal and the hardened Romanist, the eager heathen seeking light and peace for his conscience, and the cynical sceptic denying that there is any light or peace, or any need of either, for the conscience, are all being overcome by this book, and brought to the experience of the Christian faith.

We are here presented, then, with the fact that this book is laying the deepest foundation for the unification of the human race. Its adaptation to all casts of mind and all conditions of civilisation is being demonstrated beyond the possibility of intelligent denial. It is not peculiar in moulding European history, it is now making history all over the world. Of all facts upon the earth, it literally contains the deepest and strongest force which is at work amongst mankind. It is evident, then, that if any man of purely scientific interest wishes to estimate the factors.which are at work in the social evolution of to-day, he must name the Bible among the very highest. And if he is to explain these factors, is it not incumbent upon him to account for the Bible and its influence? It will not help him much, merely to investigate the authorship of its various portions and formulate theories regarding their independence or dependence on one another. What if Moses did not write the Pentateuch, or the Apostle John, the Fourth Gospel? The work which this book is doing, as a whole, remains to be accounted for as an entirely

distinct problem. Nor will it help the investigation
very much, if a man sit down and write an
elaborate treatise against the miracles of Scripture.
The fact remains still to be explained that to-day,
after eighteen hundred years of existence, the
writings of this book are the means of conferring
upon men the consciousness of fellowship with
God, and are actually giving new life to millions
of people who belong to what were considered
"decadent races." Nor will it help to say, that it
is the magnetism of the missionaries, or the touch
of a superior civilisation, or the influence of a
purer literature, that produces these results in
heathendom. The experiences which we have
described are not due finally to these causes. For
when the missionary preaches, he refers to the
Bible as his supreme authority, and he constantly
bases his teaching upon and compares his own
experience with that which is there described.
Moreover, the Bible did not come out of a civilisation which was in any great measure, if at all,
superior to that of India or of China. Nor, on the
other hand, does it help us much merely to say that
the Bible produces these effects because it is inspired.
We still want to know the relation that exists
between its substance and its effects. It must
be the substance of the book, and not its form,
its substance, and not the mere method of its
inditement, which accounts for its place and
function in that progress of man which is proceeding at so unparalleled a rate to-day. The Christian
man explains it, as we have seen already, by saying

that the Bible is that book which describes the revelation of God, and the redemption of the world ; it is that book which more clearly, more convincingly, and more powerfully than any other that could be written, presents the figure and reveals the spirit of Jesus Christ, the Lord and Saviour of the race. There is its power, there is the secret of its fascination, says the Christian man. It is the book through which now God speaks to men, because it describes God's own acts among men, for mankind. Those acts are its substance. It is as men find those acts bearing down upon their own consciences, their own affections, their own ideals, their own wills, that transformation begins.

CHAPTER V

THE close connection which exists between popular education and advanced civilisation is one of the most obvious facts which our century has brought to light. No less remarkable is the close connection which has always subsisted between the Christian faith and the work of education. No other religion appears to require education or even naturally to stimulate it. Mohammedanism, which enjoins amongst its followers a certain degree of knowledge of the teachings of the Koran, is content if these are learned by rote. Buddhism and other religions of the East possess more or less extensive religious literatures, and there are classes of people to whom these are familiar and who feel themselves under a religious necessity to read them ; but, again, none of these religions has done anything either to stimulate intellectual interest in other matters than those immediately concerned with the religious instinct, or to make the conferring of education upon the general masses of the people a religious duty. How is it that wherever Christianity, in its evangelical form, extends, the work of education inevitably goes with it ? In a land like this, where government has made the work of education an essential part of the life and growth of even the smallest communities, it seems only a matter of course to every one that the work should be done on this large scale. Few people seem to see that there exists a very close connection between, I do not say education, but *universal* education and religion. Indeed, we have become so accustomed to this idea of a universal and popular education, that we have come to deem it what we call a natural right, and we can hardly imagine the existence of a civilised government which does not give a foremost place in its work to the education of the young. The fact is, however, that we owe the popular education of modern European countries to the Christian religion. Rulers did not dream either of the possibility or the advisability, still less of the duty, of conferring it upon their subjects and citizens until after the Reformation. Then education began to spread among the people. In Germany and Scotland, especially, provision was made, before any other great nation had seen the ideal, for the establishment of local schools where the poorest might have the elements of education taught to them. And why ? Because in those countries there lived certain men who were determined to make it possible for every citizen to read the Bible. Where the Reformation was not so thorough, as in France, or where it was accompanied by the retention of a certain theory of authority and a certain doctrine of sacramental grace, as in England, there popular education spread much more slowly. Where, as in Spain and Italy, the Reformation did not penetrate, popular education has hardly been attained even to this day. Not only is it religion as such, but what we call evangelical religion, which, as a matter of history, has given the primary impulse towards the establishment of universal popular education.

I may add that, as I believe, evidence could be obtained from the history of education, even in Britain and America, to prove that in those sections of society where interest in evangelical Christianity is on the wane, the conviction of the necessity of popular education and personal interest in it begin to lose their force. Just as only a society which is nourished on the ideals of evangelical Christendom can make true democracy permanent, so sure is it that only where the same instincts are regnant will the people who manage the affairs of state continue to care much about universal education.

Moreover, it has been well said that "it is the Christian school in England, in America, in China, and in India, that is at the foundation of Christian institutions."[1] But on that fact I need not dwell.

The first explanation of this close alliance between Christianity and education will be found to lie in the facts connected with its historical origin. We shall find reason to hold that this faith cannot be maintained in its purity, except as the Bible is

[1] F. A. Noble, D.D., in *L. M. C.*, vol. ii., p. 204.

read widely and familiarly among those who believe. Now, that book describes the history of the revelation of God, and the redemption of man. It is upon these historical facts that our faith is founded. Make them dim to the mind of the individual, and his conscience, his love, his fulness of hope are made correspondingly dim and poor. He must have those words abiding in him which describe the fountains of divine life in man. He must have those great events ever present to his imagination, and subject to the scrutiny of his intellect, which opened those fountains. Hence it is, that wheresoever this gospel is preached throughout the whole world, there the hunger is awakened in all hearts for knowledge of those events, for the possession of those records, at first hand. Men and women who believe that God has done great things for them, and offered great blessings to them, yearn to have personal access to that which they are told is His own Word concerning these divine acts and these sublime promises.

But when men hitherto unlearned come to familiarity with the Bible, they find in it a collection of books, a literature possessing very great educational value and influence. There is no monotony, but rather an entrancing variety of literary forms into which its stories and revelations are cast. Moreover, there is no narrowness in the range of its influence. Every kind of human instinct has its representation here, and nearly every phase of human character and activity receives some description in connection with some

portion or another of this history of revelation.
Love and war, religious festival and regal splendour,
the woe of doubt and unbelief, the joy of faith
and divine fellowship, the temporary tragedy of
righteousness, and the final overthrow of the world's
incalculable evil, are all depicted here, often with
great dramatic force and passion.   All the elements
of human nature—its appetites and affections,
struggles and toils, sorrows and triumphs—combine
to form the rich harmonies which are heard by
him who comes to these pages with the simplicity
of faith and the aspirations of love.

And yet, again, this book gives a wider view of
the world to the poor heathen, who begins to read
it as God's word to him.   There is an outlook
upon all nations suggested, if not clearly defined, by
the earlier part of Genesis,—an outlook which may
seem at a later stage of the history almost wholly
lost, but which rises again like the sun in his
morning splendour when Christ has ascended and
His disciples contemplate a redeemed world, which
" God so loved."   It is not easy to estimate the
influence which this book, in virtue of these
characteristics, has exerted upon the race.   Whole
regions have been awakened to the beginning of
the intellectual life by this means.   Vast hosts of
humankind have been thus liberalised and ennobled by these wider conceptions, by these feelings
of personal interest in the fortunes of a people with
whom otherwise they could have had no community
of sentiment, and, above all, by that marvellous
consciousness of having been received into the

glorious brotherhood of mankind which this book confers upon the poorest citizen or the meanest tribe in the world.

But there is another point of view. The Christian faith not only rests on a history; it also implies or yields a philosophy. Jesus said, "I am the truth"; and that may be taken to mean, at least, that His teaching and the faith of His disciples are founded upon ultimate facts. Every religion does, more or less directly and intelligently, lead the mind to form conceptions regarding the relations of God and man, the origin and destiny of the world, etc. Concerning these ultimate problems the mind of man possesses an insatiable curiosity. Missionaries tell us of the eagerness with which those who first begin to read the Bible listen to its exposition, and fasten upon its teachings about creation and providence. The Christian faith, since it contains affirmations concerning God and man and the world, and their mutual relations, leads the mind right into the midst of the hardest problems which it can encounter.

These affirmations, when men begin to reason about them, are seen to constitute or suggest a philosophy. The early centuries of Church history show us the effect of thus presenting the Christian religion, as containing or implying certain great doctrines concerning the ultimate nature of things, to peoples that had for centuries discussed philosophy. What enthusiasm of thought! What widespread absorption in abstruse problems! What eagerness in the defence of the most intricate theses! And what intensity of feeling about the effect which this or that theory of God or man would produce upon the substance of Christian faith and experience! The same awakening which took place in and through the early Christian Church in Southern Europe, Northern Africa, and Western Asia, which gained further and deeper extension at the Reformation in Northern Europe, has been spreading through all the world during this century.

The missionary societies are literally the greatest educational institutions in the world, if by greatness we understand not the mere numbers who attend their schools, though these are very great, but the influence which they exert in awakening the minds of all races to the highest problems and efforts of the intellect, and the significance of their work for the future development of wide and densely populated regions of the earth. It has been said by one of themselves that missionaries " have probably devoted more time to educational work, in one form or another, than to all these others combined "; and he refers to preaching, translating, overseeing, and so forth.

Let us trace the stages through which this educational work passes in a savage land, say in the South Seas or in Africa. The missionary, as soon as he has got a few pages of the New Testament, with the alphabet, printed, finds one or more persons who are willing to learn to read. They take delight in it. Their delight is contagious, for they immediately begin to communicate to others what they have attained. As soon as possible the missionary adds to the reading of the New Testament the elements of writing and arithmetic. New enthusiasm is awakened. Old and young are eager to be taught. By this time some have learned enough to be recognised as assistant teachers, and they are appointed to class work. As neighbouring towns and villages demand teaching, suitable young men, if possible Christian men, are sent to open schools in new fields. This imposes new duties upon the missionary. He must now oversee the teachers in their various fields, and he must institute special advanced classes for the training of future teachers and evangelists. This means the preparation of more text-books, the translation of more books of geography and history, of practical religion and Bible instruction. He is now sowing the seed of a college and theological seminary. The minds of the erstwhile savage people, whose sole thought was of hunting or fishing or fighting or gardening, of sleeping and eating and quarrelling, are opened to the wider world and its interests. In the meantime commerce has increased with European and American traders, government by the chief or king has become more complex,—the people have, in fact, ceased to be a group of gregarious animals, and have taken an intelligent place in the family of mankind where their own influence is definite and palpable.

The results of the process which I have sketched are visible in the millions of people who now have the privilege of education, where fifty or sixty years ago there was no such thing as a book. The South

Sea Islands are well-nigh thoroughly covered with day schools. Madagascar had, before its occupation by the French, about one thousand schools and one hundred thousand pupils. At Antananarivo the college for educating teachers and the seminary for educating a native ministry were year by year increasing in efficiency and in the thoroughness of the intellectual training which they gave. In Africa, whether we look at the missions in the North, South, East or West, we find the same phenomenon. All the missionaries of all societies in all lands are educators. They are doing that work whose importance for the future history of the race simply cannot be estimated. No other institution is doing it in these savage lands, until, the foundations having been laid by the missionaries, the State, at some stage in the progress of civilisation, steps in and becomes responsible for it.

But let us turn to lands where, before the missionary arrived, some kind and degree of education was already enjoyed by the people. For example, look at the work of the American missionaries in the Ottoman Empire. When these men and women began work in this region, they found, indeed, that there were some schools in which Mohammedans received a mere smattering of an education and some schools in which Gregorian priests were trained. But real education there was none. The brave missionaries set themselves to supply the lack. They established not only day-schools for children, but also advanced schools which grew

into noble and high-class institutions. Robert
College at Constantinople, the colleges at Beirut
and Harpoot and elsewhere are vigorous and strong
centres of rational education. This kind of work
has been indeed bitterly opposed by those who
take a narrow view of the missionary's work and
his relation to the people among whom he lives.
President Washburn of Robert College has said:
"The attacks made upon this kind of work, although
not altogether without excuse, were undoubtedly
a mistake which put back the missionary work of
the East a quarter of a century. The result of this
interesting and noble work is that both Moslems
and Catholics have been aroused throughout the
Empire. Whereas in that Empire in 1829 there
was not one school for girls, to-day there is hardly
a town in which girls may not learn to read."
After the American schools had been in operation
for forty years, the Turkish Government did in 1869
officially promulgate school laws and institute a
scheme of governmental education. In connection
with this field of labour it has been said: "It
would take a long list to exhaust the religious,
literary, and scientific contributions to the Arabic
language from the missionaries of Syria. They
include the translation of the Scriptures and the
stereotyping of the same in numerous styles; the
preparation of a Scripture guide, commentaries, a
concordance, and a complete hymn and tune book;
text-books in history, algebra, geometry, trigo-
nometry, logarithms, astronomy, meteorology,
botany, zoology, physics, chemistry, anatomy,

physiology, hygiene, materia medica, practice of physic, surgery; and a periodical literature which has proved the stimulus to a very extensive native journalism. The Protestant converts of the mission, educated by the missionaries, have written elaborate works on history, poetry, grammar, arithmetic, natural science, and the standard dictionary of the language, and a cyclopædia which will make a library by itself, consisting of about twenty volumes of from six hundred to eight hundred pages each." [1]

Now, in all these lands, the problem of education has been comparatively simple. The path of the missionary has appeared plain and straight and inevitable. He could not be a missionary without becoming a teacher. But there are countries where the relation of the missionary to education is both intricate and perplexing. In India, above all other countries, the difficulties have been immense. True, in many parts of that great region the missionary finds himself among peoples as simple, as ignorant, as destitute of the opportunities of education as the inhabitants of Madagascar. Here the work of founding schools and training teachers goes on in the most obvious and unembarrassing manner. The real problem is connected with the attempt to evangelise the higher castes. They would enter certain schools which the Government had founded for the purpose of fitting them to use their own language in the transaction of business on behalf of the Government.

[1] Cf. Dr. Jessup, in *Missions at Home and Abroad*, pp. 258, 259.

At last the Government even went the length of providing teachers at Calcutta, to give instruction in the vernacular, the non-literary, and popular languages. But the children of these castes were found by early missionaries practically inaccessible.

It was reserved for the great Scottish missionary, Alexander Duff, to introduce that system which has done more than anything else to develop the Indian mind, and enabled it to grasp Western ideas. While yet a young man, and a comparative stranger in Calcutta, he decided that the right thing to do was to teach the higher caste Indians through the English language. His theory was scouted as an impossible dream. But he managed to put it into practice, gathered a number of youths who had at the Government schools been emancipated from their native superstitions and fears, and taught them in English. Of course, for this purpose, the native languages had to be used. Their progress was so rapid as to encourage Dr. Duff himself. At the end of a year, he invited prominent Government officers to visit his school. He conducted a public examination, and the results were so amazing, that henceforth his plan had the support of the British rulers of India. Most gratifying of all to Dr. Duff was the fact that some of the most brilliant of his earliest pupils became Christians, and exercised great influence afterward in behalf of the gospel.

Thus was begun that which is known to-day as the Christian College system in India. To the mind of its founder, Dr. Duff, it seemed to be the

case that the use of the English language and the
power to read English literature would prepare
the minds of the Indian youth very rapidly to
grasp Christian truth. He had found that it was
extremely difficult to express the doctrines of this
religion in native terms. Their languages had
been moulded by certain theories, religious and
philosophical, which were distinctly anti-Christian.
Hence it could only be with the greatest difficulty,
by coining words, or using what they had with
explanations which modified their current mean-
ings, that adequate instruction could be carried on.
Now, the English language has been moulded by the
Christian religion. Its words have been fitted by
long centuries of history to the nicest discrimina-
tions in Christian theology and philosophy. If
only, then, the Indian youths could be taught to
read the English language fluently, and to become
familiar with its modes of expression, that would
at once lift them into the intellectual atmosphere
where the gospel has lived and breathed freely for
ages. Of course, Dr. Duff made the reading of the
Bible a prominent feature of his school work, and
its teachings were fully explained. That has
remained to this day an essential part of the
work of these institutions. It is, indeed, their
raison d'être.

It must be confessed that within the Christian
Church at home, both in England and America,
there has been considerable criticism of this kind
of work. It has been urged that this is not the
evangelism for which people have subscribed their

money to the great societies, that the labour and expenditure are not justified by the number of conversions of educated young men to faith in Jesus Christ. On the other hand, it is urged that most valuable conversions have taken place, that the young men who go out of the colleges, knowing the Bible as they do, and mixing with the Christian people as they do, not only cannot longer hold their own religion, but cannot entertain the hatred for Christianity which they otherwise would have done. None in India are so dangerous to the welfare of the whole people as the youths who have grown up in Government colleges in infidelity, and who have caught the tricks of phrase and thought of the latest and most blatant opponents of religious faith in Europe and America. The most thoughtful Indians, even when they are not avowed Christians, dread this drift into infidelity. They see its immense dangers, not only to the individual youths who so drift, but to the whole structure of society against which they turn. These 'emancipated' young men have no substitute of a positive kind to offer for the customs and the faiths of their ancestors. They are mere iconoclasts, not builders of a new and fairer temple for humanity. The educated and infidel young man is felt by all who regard him thoughtfully in India, whether they are heathen or Christian, to be a social pest.

One of the ablest missionaries in India said at the London Conference in 1888: "While I am ready to admit that the spread of Western know-

ledge is powerful in pulling down old systems, and
uprooting grotesque forms of belief, the fibres of
which are subtly interlaced with the religious and
social life of the vast communities dwelling in
India, it is at the same time opening the floodgates
of infidelity, non-religion, aye, and immorality too.
For where a man's principles are not kept in check
by any acknowledgment of moral responsibility,
where the man is not awed and restrained by any
fear of coming retribution, immorality must almost
of necessity follow." The same speaker bore
witness concerning the Christian colleges: "It is
a mistake to suppose that because the Bible is
prominently taught in the mission school it is in
disfavour. The very opposite opinion and feeling
obtain. There is no institution throughout the
length and breadth of India that has drawn to it
half the popularity of the Christian College in
Madras; and, as far as academic distinction and
universal success are concerned, it outstrips every
other. The Government institutions are simply
nowhere. And yet in the Christian College the
Bible is prominently taught." Mr. Burgess then
added this significant evidence from heathen
sources of the value of the gospel in relation to
education in India: "I knew a member of the
Madras Legislative Council years ago, who daily
sent his son in a carriage and pair a mile and a
half farther than the Government institution to a
place where all religion was not ignored. I know
a Mohammedan nobleman in Hyderabad at the
present time. He was nursed in the lap of luxury;

he is learned in everything that Spencer has written ; but yet the other day, when his patronage was asked for a certain educational appointment, by an avowed atheist, he said, 'Well, if I must choose, give me the Christian with his Bible, but not the atheist in India.'"[1]

It comes to this, then, that in India men of all kinds recognise the extraordinary function which the Christian schools of every grade are exercising upon the social development of the people. For what is true of these Christian colleges, that they alone seem to give stability of character and dignity of ideals to large masses of the educated youth of India, must be true also of the thousands of Christian schools throughout the whole country. They are all at the very centre, and contain in themselves the secret and source of the progress of man throughout these teeming populations. Moreover, they manifest their impulsive power in virtue, not of that secular instruction which they give in common with secular schools, but in virtue of the religious element which is introduced by the teaching of the Bible into the life of these institutions. It is that which is proving itself the preserving and purifying salt and light in the midst of a society which, already corrupt enough, is in danger of passing downwards into deeper darkness still.

In one direction the missionary movement has stimulated a form of education which appeals to

[1] Rev. William Burgess, in *L. M. C.*, vol. i., pp. 206, 207. Cf. Rev. Wm. Miller, *ibid.*, vol. ii., pp. 234–236,

our sense of humanity in a peculiar manner. I refer to the work of medical education. Most missionaries have been able to do something towards the relief of suffering and disease. Even when they have attempted nothing difficult or intricate, their simple remedies have proved of great value. And in some instances men who had little medical training have done admirable work in this direction. But, of course, it is only since the medical missionary became thoroughly established as a necessary element in the equipment of the more important missions, that this kind of work has exercised a great educational impulse. The medical missionary aims at opening a dispensary and erecting a hospital as soon as possible. For this he needs assistants, and is compelled at once to begin the training of natives, whether they be converts or not. Sooner or later it becomes recognised that he is fitting men to go out and become practitioners in the simpler kinds of medical work. It is a fact that in all parts of the world these physician-evangelists are the pioneers of medicine. In India they have done their own share of medical education at the more important of their mission hospitals. In Turkey the medical missionaries found that there were hardly any doctors throughout the empire, and these few were worthless. Now the number of native doctors is very great, and is constantly increasing. The awakening of China to the value of Occidental experience in medicine was effected by a young medical missionary from England. In the life of

Dr. J. Kenneth Mackenzie,[1] the interesting story is told. His triumph in this direction began with his admission to the bedside of the dying wife of that great Chinese statesman, Li Hung Chang. National traditions and prejudices were torn down by the threatened loss of that patient's life. She was restored. Li Hung Chang was thereafter led to build and equip a hospital under Dr. Mackenzie's care, and there the first Chinese medical students were trained. They were received with coldness and neglect when they went out to practise. But afterwards the Government was aroused to the necessity of strenuous action, and it organised a system of medical education on a larger scale. Even in Japan, where we might have expected that the determination to learn from the Western world would have led to the opening of schools of medicine, the same phenomenon presents itself. Again it was a medical missionary who seems to have given the initial impulse. Dr. J. C. Berry made it a part of his work to convene the native doctors and give them what instructions were possible regarding more rational methods in the treatment of disease than their poor traditions had made possible. "He soon had," we are told, "a band of one hundred and twenty native doctors with him." Professional enthusiasm, thus created, led to a great desire for better and fuller training ; students were sent to Europe and America to learn medicine in the best schools, and return as the instructors and leaders of their fellow-countrymen.

[1] *John Kenneth Mackenzie*, by Mrs. Bryson.

The aim of this chapter has not been to minimise any agency of a non-Christian or a non-religious nature which is promoting education in the world. It is a fact that education has become, or is becoming, in many lands hitherto known as heathen, a function of the State, and it is of immeasurable significance. It would be foolish, for example, to compare the number of pupils in the mission schools of India with the number in the Government schools. My argument is complete, if it can be taken as proved that in practically all lands where the idea of popular education is to-day taking root, the missionary enterprise has had much or everything to do with the sowing of the seed. Even in India this has been the case. For it does not appear that the Government of India had thought of attempting the education of any native until it wished to have clerks and other officials for its own service. The establishment of the present magnificent and ever-extending system of education was due to the Christian enthusiasm of men who went out from England to be rulers of a nobler type than their predecessors had been. They co-operated with and were much influenced by great missionaries, such as Carey and Duff and Wilson. It was out of that religious atmosphere that, in spite of the opposition of the older class of officials (those representatives of the non-religious civilised man), the education of India arose.

In China, in Japan, in Madagascar the same thing has happened. When each of these lands was unsealed, and Western life poured in, the first to land, the first to settle, the first to touch the deeper sides of native life, the first to begin education were the men and women whom we know as missionaries of Christ. Now this is a fact of immense importance for every student who would fain see the inner meaning of the progress of man. Whatever that progress may be or not be, and we may have to discuss that, at anyrate it cannot exclude education. These nations of heathendom cannot be brought into the family of mankind except as they share in the education of the highest races. And here we have seen that the pioneers of education have been the men and women who went out as preachers of Christ, as the instruments of the highest and purest religious force in history.

CHAPTER VI

THE MISSIONARY AND SELF-SACRIFICE—THE VALUE OF MARTYRDOM

THAT which most impressed the churches in the early part of this century was the heroism and self-sacrifice of the Christian missionary. When Carey or Judson went out to the East from their homelands with a mere pittance of money at their disposal, with no security as to salary, they manifested a courage that amazed all. When they cast themselves against the enormous difficulties of the work of evangelisation, their dauntless faith and determination could not but evoke both amazement and admiration. No one had preceded them upon whose experience they could draw. They had to fight their way through all prejudices, through the obstacles created both by Europeans and natives. They had to discover the best ways of approaching the native mind and character, to ponder and to decide how best to deal alike with the heathen, who were willing to listen to them, and the converts who were willing to confess Jesus Christ. And far on into the century a considerable part of the interest in foreign missions was created

or increased by the feeling of admiration which all
had for those who left home and comfort to live
among cannibals in the South Seas or to pass into
the dark parts of Africa.   They all possessed the
devotion of spirit expressed in the prayer of one
living missionary, who in his youth knelt down
and prayed that God would send him into the
darkest place on the earth.   When such men left
home in those years, it was for good.   The idea of
a regular furlough was not in their minds; the
immense dangers by sea and land, from human
savages and savage beasts, were all in their minds.
And many a young man or woman, in saying farewell, said it as those do who go out to face the
almost certain death of a fierce campaign.   In
those days, as I have said, the heroism and self-
sacrifice were so obvious and great that no one
questioned their supreme significance.

   But in our day one hears a considerable amount
of speech somewhat derogatory of this self-
sacrifice.   On the one hand, good and earnest
missionaries themselves have come home and have
denied that they made any sacrifice.   They have
said that the honour and the joy of the work were
so great as to obliterate from their minds the feeling that they had lost or sacrificed anything
comparable with these, by entering the missionary
career.   And a good many people who have no
heart themselves to follow that example are
beginning to echo these words of saintly self-
sacrifice, and to speak as if it were the bare fact
that the missionary life is not one of supreme

sacrifice.   Then this matter is discussed from another point of view, when men compare the life of the missionary with that of the soldier, the trader, the traveller, or the civil servant.   All these, it is said, leave their homeland; bid farewell to their dear ones; go forth to dangers of sea and land; live among savage and degraded peoples; part with their children, sending them home for education; encounter the inconveniences, the sicknesses, and the sorrows incidental to residence in lands like those.   What does the missionary do more than these, it is asked?   Why not speak of *their* self-sacrifice, and hail it with gratitude?

The result of movements of feeling and thought like this is, that in various directions it comes to be taken for granted, that the missionary career should not now be encircled with the halo of the martyr, nor be renowned for heroic qualities of unique or surprising degree.   On this whole matter the following observations seem to contain some value.   In the first place, no one would care to depreciate the heroism involved in many of the secular careers above referred to.   They have manifested a certain kind of bravery, a resourcefulness, and even self-control.   They do stand for something in the progress of man; they have exerted, merely as examples of heroism, a true influence upon the life of the race.   The whole world is the better for manifestations of daring, of devotion to a purpose and skill in its pursuit, which these various classes of men have given to us all.

That which we wish to ask is not, *at first*, whether the courage of the missionary or his self-sacrifice has been equal to that of any other class of men, but whether a difference of motive does not impart a difference of quality to self-sacrifice in such careers. Does the trader, who sails to the South Seas to stay there for ten years, buying and selling and making gain, manifest self-sacrifice in the same way as the missionary, who goes to the same islands and settles down also for ten years to be the teacher and saviour of the natives? Do we not all feel and see that the difference of aim has imparted a difference of quality to the sacrifice of self involved in the courage of these two men respectively? Of course it does. The missionary has not only given himself up once for all to the service of Jesus Christ—the other may have done that—he has, further, resolved to cut himself off from all desire for wealth or fame or earthly promotion, and to give himself in that distant island, body and heart and mind, wholly and without reserve, to the interests of those degraded people. It is his life, himself, that he is giving to them. Not so the trader. He may be a good man, quite up to the ordinary standards of Christian goodness; he may even take a benevolent interest in the work of the missionary. But his leaving of the homeland, though it cost tears and pangs, has not gone so to the depths of his nature, because it did not of itself involve that further sacrifice of self which the missionary has made. So it is with the traveller or the soldier or

the civil servant. These men avowedly seek glory
and honour for themselves, for their work; and
the sacrifice of home has been made, not with a
view to the deeper sacrifice of self in those lands,
but to the gaining of a higher earthly self, to the
attainment of a position whose glory shall be reflected
far and near, as the glory of this man or that man.

But now I believe that there is also a great
difference in degree as well as in quality between
the self-sacrifice of these various classes of men
and that of the missionary ; there is an immeasurable gulf separating the whole attitude of mind
and heart in which the missionary and these
others stand towards the natives amongst whom
they live. The missionary is face to face with
these natives, with the burden of their individual
souls upon him. It is his task to open his thought
and feeling to all the impressions of horror and
sadness and despair, which his contact with
idolatry and immorality and ignorance and dead-
ness of heart make upon him. When he views
these native customs, it is not as the ethnologist
purely and simply, not as the mere observer and
recorder of sociological facts, but as the tender
soul upon whom each and all of these facts bring
grief. He lives a life of peculiar loneliness, as a
rule. He stands face to face with degradation and
darkness. He sees the trader succeeding in his
work, and the traveller marching rapidly to glory
and a book of many editions, and he can sympa-
thise with them, but hardly they with him.
Seldom has he the joy of intercourse with a human

heart outside his own home, which can understand
the burden of souls which he bears. Yet more,
the missionary has to identify himself so completely with the people for whom he labours that
he comes to love them as if he were one of them.
Few missionaries have left a field where they have
laboured many years without the deepest pangs
of regret. Listen to a missionary from Madagascar, or from India, or even from some humbler
tribe in Africa, speak of his field and his people,
of the problems lying before them, of their
prospects as a race, of the triumphs of the gospel
among them, and you will always feel that you
are looking into a heart ablaze with love itself. I
know of no love in the world so like that of Jesus,
so obviously a reflection of that central sun of
love, the Heart of the Eternal, as this love of
the missionary of the nineteenth century for the
people that he is winning to Christ. It must be
obvious that such love costs what cannot be
measured, as all brooding, parental, redeeming
love does.

And then we must speak, not only of lives of
sacrifice, but of deaths. Who can number the
missionaries that lie dead in far-off fields? How
many of these died in early youth of fevers and
pestilences?   Many will, no doubt, remember
Professor Henry Drummond's description of the
mission station at Livingstonia in Central Africa.
There, " on the silver sand of a small bay stood the
small row of trim white cottages. A neat path
through a small garden led up to the settlement,

and I approached the largest house and entered."
He passed through several, "And so on to the next,
and the next, all in perfect order, and all *empty*.
Then a native approached me and led me a few
yards into the forest.   And there among the
mimosa trees, under a huge granite mountain,
were four or five graves.   These were the missionaries."[1]   When Alexander Mackay bade farewell
to the committee of his society, before leaving
with some other young men for Central Africa, he
said, "Is it at all likely that eight Englishmen
should start for Central Africa and all be alive six
months after?   One of us at least—it may be I—
will surely fall before that.   But what I want to
say is this: when the news comes, do not be cast
down, but send some one else immediately to take
the vacant place."[2]   In the same spirit M. Golaz,
a young French missionary, when dying within
one year of his arrival in Senegambia, spoke thus:
"Do not be discouraged if the first labourers fall
in the field.   Their graves will mark the way for
their successors, who will march past them with
great strides."[3]

Many missionaries have fallen by the hand of
the assassin.   No doubt among the other classes
mentioned above, who live and work in heathen
lands, multitudes have died, and many have been
slain.   But there is one feature connected with the

[1] *Tropical Africa*, p. 41.   One of the most pathetic scenes in
missionary history will be found described in *Ten Years North of
the Orange River*, by John Mackenzie, chap. x.
[2] *Mackay of Uganda*, p. 32.
[3] *Vide The Gospel Message*, by R. N. Cust, LL.D., pp. 45-62.

murder of missionaries which we do not find
manifested when any other class of men is put to
death. It is this, that no missionary, so far as I
have ever heard, fights for his life. He will
escape, if he can; he will use persuasion and all
other straightforward and legitimate means of
escape, but he will not lift his hand to slay his
assailant. It is not to their shame that the
wounds of many dead missionaries have been in
their backs. They have had guns with them,
but have not used them against even the most
malignant foes. They have followed the example
of Jesus in this matter, as He may have intended
that all His disciples should follow it to the utter-
most. They have persistently loved their enemies,
and done good to those that cursed them, and
prayed for those that despitefully used them,
and cried not for vengeance but for mercy upon
those who put them and their families to slaughter.
The ordinary soldier or trader or traveller does
not believe in allowing himself to be put to death
by a "cursed nigger" without resistance, and,
if possible, vengeance. Even Christian men of
undoubtedly high character have not scrupled to
slay their assailants, although they knew that
resistance was of no avail. For example, of one
civil servant in India, described as a "godly
judge" and "a brave official," it is said that when
he found himself, in the time of the Indian Mutiny,
surrounded by Mohammedans seeking his life,
"having read the comfortable words of Scripture
and having commended himself to God, he brought

out all the arms he had and prepared to defend his life. . . . Summoned to abjure Christ and accept Mohammed, he resolutely refused. As the police guard (the mutineers) advanced, he shot fourteen or sixteen of these — the accounts vary — before he fell, confessing Christ." "Robert Tucker," Dr. George Smith adds, "was the glory of the Bengal Civil Service, and he was not alone in his heroism or his confession."[1]

The martyr spirit which has thus been manifested by the missionaries of the nineteenth century has been communicated to the converts whom they have made. It is impossible to realise the amount of suffering and sacrifice which has been incurred by those who have confessed Christ throughout heathendom. The earliest confessors have almost invariably become the objects of ridicule and hostility from their own countrymen. In some parts of the world this time of open persecution has, indeed, passed rapidly away. In the islands of the Pacific, where the idols were cast aside over and over again by a public tribal resolution and act, the penalties involved in submitting to baptism have not been prolonged or severe. And yet one of the most remarkable facts connected with the spread of Christianity in those islands has been the heroism with which the converts, as soon as they gained sufficient education, have been willing to devote their lives to the work of evangelisation in other islands. The great progress which has been made in New Guinea during the last twenty

[1] *Life of Dr. Duff*, vol. ii., p. 344.

years would have been impossible without the assistance of native evangelists from other islands already Christianised. No European or American missionary could have excelled some of these in the courage with which they have faced fever and assassination, far from their own homes, sometimes in utter loneliness amongst fierce and cannibal tribes.

The difficulties which lie before every man or woman in India who would confess Christ are now thoroughly known to us all. We know how the caste system has surrounded with peculiar horror the act of receiving baptism; how the poor youth who cannot deny his love for Jesus Christ is treated as one who has degraded himself and his whole family in the eyes of the community. He must tear himself sometimes from the clasp of a mother's arms, whose pleadings and tears have been applied to soften his heart and whose shrieks of bitterness follow him into his life of homelessness. Such men have been spat upon by their wives, have heard their children told to curse them, have been disinherited and sent out poor and naked and bruised into the world. Many have been put to death.

Where men of promise and position have become Christians, as in the case of Khama, one of the leading chiefs of South Africa, they have been compelled to face persecution after another fashion. The story of this confessor is now well known. For refusing to marry more than one wife or to take any part in the native practices of witchcraft,

to which as heir to the chieftainship he ought to
have been given, this man and his brother were
openly driven from the town and attacked with
arms by their heathen and dark-hearted father.
While as Christians they could not yield to his
evil will, as Christians they refused to lift a hand
against him, except in self-defence. Entrenching
themselves with the Christian party of the tribe in
a strong position, outside the town, they simply
fought when attacked.   By maintaining an attitude
of noble patience, of quiet dignity, by revealing
the purity of his motives, the tenderness of heart,
and at the same time the strong will of a born
ruler, this man at last himself became chief, and
has made his mark in the history of the development of South Africa.   Everywhere on the mission
field, which now practically means throughout
the world, the same old martyr 'spirit has been
revealed in thousands and tens of thousands of
cases, as that of which we read with bated breath
and worshipful awe in the early Church or in the
times of the Reformation.   And to-day it is
proved that the ancient saying of the brave Latin
father is true, that the blood of the martyrs is the
seed of the Church.   When every missionary was
driven from Madagascar, and a reckless queen
sought to exterminate the gospel by slaying two
thousand of her own subjects, she really only increased the number of Christian believers.   In
India the awful Mutiny broke out and was directed
towards the destruction of the Christian Churches;
many Christian pastors and teachers as well as

missionaries were put to death. The chief result
of this effort was, that during the decades that
followed the Mutiny, Christianity spread at a rate
far surpassing that of other periods.

One feature of missionary work ought not, in
this connection, to be passed over without more
emphasis than I have given it. There has always
been, and there probably always will be, an element
of sorrow in the service of man. The great teachers
and reformers of the past have not slept on beds
of roses, nor found life pass like a bright summer
breeze. The progress of man is no easy process,
with banners waving and music leading the
marchers in steady and strong strides. The price
paid by human hearts for human progress is
infinite ! Those who through faith have subdued
kingdoms, wrought righteousness, obtained promises,
have always paid a bitter price for these conquests
and the privilege of this glorious labour. They
have indeed obtained a good report. We now say
of them, that the world was not worthy. But, alas !
the men for whom they immediately laboured did
not say it. Missionaries do not deal in their
reports and home speeches with this side of their
life. But I fancy he must have a strange life and
a strange sphere who has been a missionary and
not sorrowed through and for his work. I shall
never forget, as a youth, bidding farewell to one
man of whom the world has heard little, when he
went back to his apparently hopeless field among
the Matabele people in South Central Africa.
When Mr. Sykes turned his back upon his native

land, with his years increasing and his distaste for travelling accentuated by the years, he knew that he was leaving home for the last time. He had already worked five-and-twenty years amongst a people not easily surpassed anywhere for their brutality of life, and he had not baptised one convert. As I spoke with him, and heard his humble words of determination and even of love for his life's task, and saw the love soften his face, I felt the thrill of having spoken with a man whom one could not but call in the deepest and highest sense of the words " a heroic soul." His martyrdom lasted a lifetime. Similarly, one could not speak with James Gilmour of Mongolia, as I did, during his last brief visit home, and remember the kind of life he had been living in Mongolia, and the cheerlessness and loneliness to which he was about to return, without profound emotion. It is this kind of work which is lifting the world everywhere. By no other kind is man lifted. Progress, if, as we have said before, it has to do fundamentally with character, must then always, everywhere, at home and abroad, inevitably mean struggle, sacrifice, conquest. Every lift must cause some great strain to some one heart. No habitual sin is repressed, no social shame is abolished, no individual vice is overcome anywhere without pain. They are the promoters of the evolution of man who, having conquered self, are teaching others to do the same; who, having submitted their whole nature to the control of the Spirit of God, give up life itself, to teach others that through the same act they, too, may mount nearer unto heaven. At home, where we are surrounded by what we call, and what is largely, a Christian civilisation, these facts strike us not so clearly; yet it is true, and can be demonstrated, that here too the men who do aught for the real uplifting of our race suffer for it and work through sorrow. But on the mission field you can see this awful and wondrous law operating openly and continually. There you can imagine, when the missionary has begun to mould the thoughts of some, and the new life is beginning to shake the foundations of ancient wrongs,—you can almost imagine that every tear washes some stain away, that every sigh of the faithful heart helps to swell the breeze of heaven which is blowing the clouds of thick darkness away.

I would not have these facts leave the impression on any mind that the career of the missionary is all pain, all darkness, all struggle. I have named them, described them, emphasised them, because it is through these that the progress of man is being secured. But no less is it true that there is a brighter side to the missionary's life. The brightness does not diminish the reality of the darkness, the joy does not diminish the value of the martyrdom. But it is there,—evidence that the missionary is living on the right lines, and that under all the sorrow, all the discord that enter into his life through the kind of work that he is doing, there is a real harmony, a deep source of peace. For example, be it noted that his kind of life and his very devotion to it react on the missionary himself. Face to face there with all that denies God, the missionary casts himself the more completely upon God, and realises more profoundly the characteristic experiences of the Christian life. With nothing around him to encourage his faith, he must have recourse to a deep and more constant communion with God. The inward force of spiritual facts must be multiplied in strength, in clearness, in truth, in beauty, for the nourishing of his own faith and the filling of his hope. It was a young medical missionary in China who wrote home to his father, saying, "Out here, where I am much alone, I get to know, I am thankful to say, more of Christ as a personal Saviour." [1]

Other facts of a more material kind enter into his experience. He goes out sometimes as a man of comparatively limited intellectual training, with little more than the average interests and attainments of the ministry, and he is plunged into conditions which arouse, not only his whole spiritual, but his whole intellectual nature to activity. The very task of learning a new language, or languages, and doing so far more thoroughly than almost any ordinary minister learns any language, except his own, mastering all matters of idiom and pronunciation,—this alone is sufficient so to train his mind, as to confer upon him the very substance of that which we call culture.

Yet again, as he faces the conditions of society around him and realises that it is his task, by

[1] *John Kenneth Mackenzie*, p. 68.

God's grace, to transform these; as the actual
work takes shape and form before him, and he
must organise in this direction and in that, he
finds himself dealing with facts of a greater and
more momentous kind than any of those which
engage the mind of the average minister at home.
He is forced to become a statesman. He must
study the laws of the land, the organisation of
society, and in many cases must himself deal with
the reconstruction of these. For a man with high
and noble possibilities in him, all this must afford
a deep and true satisfaction.

And, lastly, there is the joy of the missionary,
as he sees his own great work succeeding. Who
knows but the man who has been through it, what
it is to baptise the first convert, to gather with a
few for the first time around the table of the Lord's
Supper, to listen to the first song and prayer of
family worship in a native home, to hear a native
begin to teach his fellows to read, or the first
evangelist open his mouth to preach the gospel of
Jesus Christ. When the missionary is a man
absorbed, first and last, in prayer and labour and
hope for these as the highest results of all his
efforts,—and how few there have been of whom
this is not true,—it may be said that his joy on
such occasions is a joy unspeakable and full of
glory.

At one time it was thought self-evident that
martyrdom is a direct proof of the truth of the
Christian religion. It was urged that the fact
that men and women were willing to offer their

lives and endure untold agonies for the sake of the gospel is in itself enough to establish the reality of the revelation in whose name they suffered. In recent years there has been a tendency to disparage this appeal to the witness of martyrs for confirmation of the Christian faith, and people have gone to the other extreme. It is now very commonly alleged that martyrdom proves nothing; that all kinds of superstition have had their martyrs; that if only excitement enough is aroused, many people will die for the most despised forms of doctrine. .The Hindu is pointed out as on the whole a willing sufferer, through his prolonged acts of self-mutilation or self-denial, in the pursuit of his religious ideal. He will deform his body, allow hooks to be passed through his back for the horrible swinging festival, in the enthusiasm of his religious faith. Yet, again, the Mohammedan will gladly rush on death with the cry of " Allah " upon his lips, assured that if he die for the sake of his religion he will pass immediately into the paradise of sensual joy. Yet, again, the internal history of the Christian Church itself is furnishing evidence that martyrdom proves nothing, for there the opposing parties have often been willing to sacrifice their lives in the defence of the doctrines which they respectively defended. Romanists and Protestants alike have gone into the flames or laid their heads upon the executioner's block. How then, it is urged, in the face of facts like these, can it be argued by any man who is abreast of the thought of his day, that the history of the martyrdoms which have accompanied the spread of the gospel is of any value in determining the truth or the untruth of the Christian or of any other form of belief ?

To begin with, I must confess to a feeling of distrust regarding any and every tendency to decry any of the great characteristics of human history as being worthless. I do not think that the self-immolations of the Hindu are valueless, nor that the passionate devotion of the Mohammedan stands for nothing in the evolution of man, nor that the devotion of opposing parties within the Christian Church has not been necessary to the development of the race. It seems too easy to push aside all the sacrifices of mankind on behalf of their religious ideals, as being mere superstition or mere enthusiasm or merely hysterical, and therefore unworthy of scientific investigation. This class of phenomena must be taken more seriously than it has been, and investigated on a wide scale with sympathetic interest, ere there can be a chance of doing justice to it and its influence in history. In the first place, we must distinguish between the various classes of martyrdom which have occurred in the history of religion. It is evident, for example, that the wild enthusiasm of the Mohammedan, which invariably takes the form of the intoxication of battle, is distinct from the spirit of either the Hindu devotee or the Christian martyr. The Mohammedan is not taught that he will gain paradise for mere martyrdom ; he must fight, and fighting, die for his faith. His is not the meek and quiet spirit that endureth all things, because it loves all men. It contains no ethical element [1] except that of determination to win a physical paradise, and, if necessary, to kill as many human beings as possible in the effort.

And then, as regards the Hindu, one cannot but see in such profound self-denial a fact of real value. His martyrdom, although self-inflicted, is not worthless, is not to be swept aside as the blind and unreasoning outcome of an ignorant and baseless superstition. Is it not the expression of his profound sense of the reality of the ideal life, whose ·glory is so great, though he but dimly see it and feel after it and know not when he has found it, that he will give up all else for that? The Mohammedan merely wants another world, another and longer life, like this. The Hindu or the Buddhist devotee stands amongst men as a wonderful witness to the infinite value of the spiritual world, into which the physical and the sensual enter not, for hearts that have caught the vision of its reality.

As regards the martyrdoms that have arisen in the course of the struggles between the parties in the Christian Church, we must be careful again to distinguish. Some of these have a religious significance which is immediate and evident, while some have been the expression simply of devotion to a

---

[1] "All the acts of soldiers in a holy war will be considered as prayer, and the martyrs will go to paradise without an examination into their lives"—this was said by the Sheik-ul-Islam, "the highest authority possible," and quoted by President Washburn in *The Outlook* (N.Y.), vol. lvi., p. 743.

party or to a national ideal. Where patriotism or partisanship has entered in, they must be estimated after the same fashion as we estimate the significance for the human race of the soldier's devotion to his country. Where these martyrdoms have contained true Christian or religious significance has been where those who suffered, whether heretic or orthodox, Romanist or Protestant, believed sincerely that the doctrine for which they contended had an essential connection with the central facts of the Christian faith and experience, as such. They may have been wrong on either side, sometimes on both sides; but so far as they seemed to themselves to see a vital connection between specific doctrines and the very essence of the Christian religion, their martyrdom must be considered as belonging to the same class as the martyrdoms of those who suffered for the faith at the hands of heathen men.

What, then, have been those elements in the sacrifice of Christian martyrs which distinguish them from sacrifices made by all other religious devotees? The following observations may be taken as, I hope, not incorrect and not without some important bearing upon the problem before us.

1. In the first place, let the case of the Christian martyrdoms be stated thus: Throughout these nineteen hundred years innumerable individuals have been put to torture and death on account of their faith by their own tribal or national authorities. The torture is not of their choosing; it is

9

inflicted upon them; and this not amid the excitement of battle, but in cold blood, before the eyes of thousands of onlookers, or in lonely dungeons and secret chambers of horror. In accepting the Christian faith they have, as individuals, broken away from all the traditions and customs of their people. They have laid themselves open to the derision and contempt of their fellow-countrymen, of all whom they count dear. In many cases they have stood alone, unsupported by any sympathy from any other human being. In suffering they endured all that was done to them without resistance. In these particulars, as it seems to me, the Christian martyrs are so entirely separated either from the warlike devotion of the Mohammedan or the self-inflicted pains of the Indian devotee as to necessitate their being put into a class by themselves, that the nature and significance of their function in history may be understood and studied on their own merits. It is the shallowest conceivable method to group them all together and to pass a contemptuous judgment on them, saying that people will die for any superstition, that the appetite for martyrdom spreads like contagion, and that the history of Christian martyrdom is valueless for that reason. There are species of martyrdom which should be studied separately as well as comparatively, and of these the Christian martyrdom seems to be specifically distinct from all other forms known to history.

2. It is of great importance to observe, that this course of persecution has characterised the introduction of Christianity into nearly every nation

and tribe upon the earth. Wheresoever this religion
has gone it has aroused a deep hostility toward
itself. And those who have broken away from
their native religions and become its adherents
have, practically without exception, been compelled
to pay a bitter price for the transference of their
allegiance from idols and fetishes and Mohammed
to the name of Jesus Christ.

3. Wheresoever these martyrdoms have been
endured they have, again I must say almost invariably, led to an extension of the Christian faith
among the masses of the people, and even among
the persecutors and executioners themselves. "The
blood of the martyrs is the seed of the Church,"
is one of those utterances which have become pro-
verbial, because universal experience proves them
true. Again, it seems not only the easiest but the
least satisfactory way of accounting for this
phenomenon to say that the sight of suffering
produces a reaction of excitement amongst the onlookers and executioners, and arouses in them a
willingness to enter upon the same experience.
Enthusiasm is indeed contagious. The enthusiasm
of the veteran kindles ardour in the shrinking
heart of the recruit as they rush towards battle.
The enthusiasm of a great orator will inflame the
hearts of a great multitude for some great cause.
It is a familiar fact that crowds are easily swayed,
that the same people who at one time are filled with
insatiable desire for a king's blood may, by means
of a clever retort or some act which sets in motion
a wave of sympathy through their hearts, swing

their fickle feelings to the opposite pole, and they are ready to shout, "Long live the king!" But I have yet to see a successful exposition of the psychological steps through which the seeing of men under torture awakens a desire in the observers for the same experience. We do not read that when Eastern potentates caused their captives to be slain in their presence, any other people were willing to become captives on the same terms. There must be something in the sight of Christian martyrdom, giving it that strange power which for nineteen hundred years it has manifested in every part of the world, amongst all kinds of human beings, which is not to be found in other forms of religious self-sacrifice.

4. When Christian martyrs have suffered they have often seemed to triumph. The rule has been that they have carried themselves calmly and bravely, and have manifested a serene joy and spoken of a certain hope which filled their hearts even in the midst of darkest physical distress. This hope must not be confused with the burning passion of the Mohammedan. There have been spurious Christian martyrdoms, wherein some men appear to have cherished expectations somewhat resembling the sensuous. But we must not judge any movement by its spurious imitations, but by its normal type; and the normal typical attitude of the Christian martyr is presented in his hope of immediate admission to the presence of Jesus Christ. The whole motive of his life is summed up in that name, and the whole glory that he sees before him,

even through the martyr flames, or up beyond the circles of the amphitheatre in the blue heavens, finds its fullest expression in the apostolic longing to be with Christ. Now, whether this hope is rational or not, it must, as one that has exercised so large a place in the history of the Christian centuries, receive scientific justice. Its nature must be understood in distinction from whatever other motives have made men willing to endure suffering and death.

5. Along with this joyous hopeful spirit, the martyrs have, as a rule, and certainly in all those cases where their martyrdom has proved fruitful, manifested a spirit of purity and kindness and patience towards their persecutors and the world at large. They have not striven to resist by shedding the blood of their enemies. They have not looked at these with hatred or scorn, but only with calm dignity, sometimes with tender pity. They have gazed as from a superior level upon the very men who judged them, and spoken mercy to the poor creatures who were used as the instruments of their execution. This purity, sympathy, lovingness of spirit must be closely connected in our minds with that faith in the God of Jesus Christ for which they died. We have seen in other pages that in their religion, morality and religion were not indeed identified but unified. Here for the first time in history the religious and the ethical have become indissoluble. The relation of the believer to the Saviour is an ethical one, because it is personal. It involves him instantly in obligations towards his

Master, whose fulfilment is seen in the new character which he wears. The relationship is religious, because it is the dependence of a creature upon the Creator, of a sinful man upon the Saviour; but it is ethical, because it involves him in obligations of a definite and indisputable kind. And there, in the martyr's face, this union shines. He looks up, and it is with a religious hope; he looks round, and it is with a forgiving love. And the one name of Jesus Christ explains both the new religion and its indissoluble partner, the new morality.

6. Now as to the communication of the martyr's faith to others. It seems to be capable of a very clear and definite proof, that the elements which have, at anyrate in the vast majority of cases, attracted the interest or awakened the faith of the persecutors, have been the expression and look of religious enthusiasm, and the new ethical qualities manifested even in cruel death by these sufferers. These features of human experience, when presented to the conscience of those who saw them, amid much horror, have awakened that insatiable hunger after the same condition of heart and life. It seems, in fact, not to have been the flames but the personal qualities of the sufferers that attracted the enthusiasm of the crowds; the patience, the love, the purity, as well as the confidence and the hope of those whom they watched in martyrdom, have convinced men that this is not mere physical excitement, that this phenomenon could only be explained by a wondrous experience, whose beauty and glory were revealed in the new light which

shone out of their souls. That which results, then, when the spread of the Christian religion through martyrdoms is normal from the Christian point of view, is not that those who become converts immediately thirst for martyrdom and themselves seek the flames. They do nothing of the sort. *They go away with guilty consciences to Christian teachers, and learn of them.* They have been pierced to the quick of the deeper man, and determined to attain that condition of conscience and will which they saw in those martyrs; they persist in learning until they too have won this faith in Christ, and until in them this religious relationship has produced those ethical qualities which always flow from it, and which, so far as the heathen world knows, have flowed from it alone. Always from first to last the phenomena connected with the expansion of this religion are spurious, are disowned by the religion itself and its wiser adherents, are found in the longrun to affect others with anything but sympathy and devotion, unless this ethical element is evident in the lives alike of those who bear witness and those who through their witness, whether in life or death, become convinced and converted.

The ordinary notion that martyrdom spreads through the awakening of a kind of physical excitement will not bear the test of comparison with any actual instances. Take the case of the persecution in Madagascar, to which reference has been made. Can it be maintained that when that first sufferer, a young girl of attractive appearance, asked to be allowed to pray, and was speared as she knelt on the ground, that that scene was likely to arouse a desire in the minds of others to kneel there and be speared in their turn? Yet that was the beginning of a magnificent series of martyrdoms in that land. We are not told that the people who witnessed those dreadful events tried to get themselves killed. That which we are told is, that more and more inquirers came forward who besought the Christians to teach them the secret of the new life which they were so manifestly living. Or let us look at the extraordinary story of the conversion of Uganda. The work of putting down the new religion began with the burning of three boys aged sixteen, fourteen, and twelve years respectively. They had never seen, perhaps never heard of, a martyrdom, and they could not be induced to give up their new faith. When challenged by some of the executioners, we are told that they raised their young voices in a Christian hymn. The effect of their demeanour, and that of others who followed them to the martyr's death, was such that some even of the executioners became Christians. Why and how was this? Not because a wave of excitement was making the stake popular, which is what some would have us believe. On the contrary, when their turn came, these men and women naturally and rightly did their best to escape. For example, when a certain man who had been sent out by the king to collect tribute from a subject tribe returned, he was met with the pleasant news that he was to be slain for his faith in Christ. He did not rejoice. On the contrary, he shrank in a very healthy fashion from a violent death. Nevertheless, he carried his royal master's treasure to the palace, lest it should be said a Christian had been unfaithful to his trust, and *then* precipitately fled for his life. All the deaths of violence in Uganda had not made him even "half in love" with death, as Keats said the nightingale had made him. The martyrs would seem to have drawn men to the Christian faith, because in the moment of death these heroes made it plain that they had received a new experience so real, so glorious, that they were willing to give up all rather than deny Him from whose love they have all always believed it had come. That executioner in Uganda, who hurried to the missionary as an earnest inquirer, had seen in those victims of his an experience which he longed to possess. His sense of need was aroused. His conscience was made quick. A nobler man was beginning to stir in his brutish heart.

That is how the Church has spread through martyrdom, from the beginning of its history till now. Who will say that such phenomena appearing constantly, everywhere, for nineteen centuries, prove nothing?

7. In fine, let it be repeated that the change of character which, I believe, above all else has given the martyrs of the Christian Church their influence over the world, has been always in their own minds allied with, and has by all Christian

people been felt and said to depend upon, that
condition of pardon, of union with God, which
they attain through faith in Jesus Christ. Approach the problem of the spread of Christianity
from whatever point we may, study its influence
upon society from any aspect, we are always
brought face to face with this, that the Christian
religion develops all its life, all its ethical influence,
and manifests all its purifying power in the human
race, from this condition of fellowship with God,
which all Christians say that they receive through
faith in Jesus Christ.

CHAPTER VII

ONE hears from various critics of the missionary movement the expression of two ideas which one cannot call anything but superstitious. They are criticisms not founded upon accurate observation of the facts, either in connection with the lives of the savages or with the effects of the introduction of the Christian religion.

The first of these asserts that the savage is, on the whole, an innocent, simple-hearted, and happy being. The severe morality of the Christian religion is supposed to enter as a disturber of the peace upon the calm and satisfaction of savage life. This sentimental criticism is only made by a certain class of people, who have exercised considerable influence in recent years, the same class of people who have preached art for art's sake, and the substitution of what is called "Hellenism" for Christianity. It is all superstition; they simply do not know the facts. A man who will go into a truly heathen village, almost anywhere, will find such customs and barbarities as will make his blood run cold. Not to speak of the fearful degradation which reigned over the South Sea Islands and New Guinea when cannibalism was practised ; if we only go to the tribes of South Africa, we shall find sufficient of shame and bitterness and murder and rapine to dispel for ever that vision of the peaceful and innocent savage which some have tried to cherish. The actual morality of heathenism is indescribable. Nowhere in heathenism does society as such cast a stigma upon the liar or the cheat. The murderer may be avenged, but not by law, only by the vengeance of the relatives of his victim. As for what we understand by purity, it is simply undreamt of, even as a possibility, far less conceived of as a law incumbent upon individuals. Mrs. Bishop, the well-known traveller, says: "Missionaries come home and refrain from shocking audiences by recitals of the awful sins of the heathen and heathen world. When travelling in Asia, it struck me very much, how little we heard, how little we knew, as to how sin is cultivated, and deified, and worshipped." [1]

The same remarkable traveller and observer has made the following authoritative statements regarding the conditions of home life in lands which we are accustomed to speak of as possessing a certain degree of civilisation: "I have lived in zenanas and harems, and have seen the daily life of the secluded women, and I can speak from bitter experience of what their lives are—the intellect dwarfed, so that the woman of twenty or thirty years of age is more like a child of eight intel-

[1] *Heathen Claims and Christian Duty*, by Mrs. Bishop.

lectually; while all the worst passions of human nature are stimulated and developed in a fearful degree—jealousy, envy, murderous hate, intrigue, running to such an extent that in some countries I have hardly ever been in a woman's house or near a woman's tent without being asked for drugs with which to destroy the favourite wife, to take away her life, or to take away the life of the favourite wife's infant son. This request has been made of me nearly two hundred times. This is only an indication of the daily life of whose miseries we think so little, and which is a natural product of the system that we ought to have subverted long ago."[1]   I shall not waste time in proving that what is true of the Orientals is true, at least as true, of less civilised people.

The second superstition consists in the idea that, if only the missionary would let well alone, the effects of contact with higher forms, i.e. European and American forms of civilisation, would gradually give new personal and social ideals to the heathen world, and civilisation pure and simple would raise the condition of the heathen world to the political, industrial, and family attainments of what we call Christendom. Again, it must be said that such a theory can only be cherished by those who ignore the facts. The testimony as to the effects of contact between a higher and a lower civilisation as such, is nowadays almost superabundant, and it is painful in the extreme to any true lover of mankind. In no single case is it favourable to the

[1] *Ibid.*, p. 9.

theory which I have stated. Throughout the world the contact of the heathen peoples with civilisation has been through the three avenues of war, commerce, and Christianity. Nowhere has European civilisation communicated itself to lower races simply through the first two, conquest and trade; rather must it be said that the tendency of these two species of communion between the higher and the lower has invariably been towards the destruction of the lower races. The trader, with a few noble exceptions, has not been a man, either in Africa or the South Sea Islands or in the Orient, whose influence tended to raise the character of those with whom he dealt; and the conquerors, the soldiers, and governors of these peoples were not, until the close of the first quarter of this century, men who gave much thought or care to the uplifting of those from whom they exacted the homage of subjects. In fact, it is notorious that these representatives of civilisation have, as a rule, lived lives which would have brought upon them disgrace and ostracism from all decent society in their homelands. Where they have come into contact with missionary operations, the natives have in thousands of cases pointed the finger of scorn at them and said to the missionaries: Are these the products of your Christian religion? Hence, one may with every confidence quote the strong affirmation of the Rev. James Chalmers, one of the noblest of living missionaries: "I have had twenty-one years' experience amongst natives. I have seen the semi-civilised and the uncivilised; I have lived with the Christian native, and I have lived, dined, and slept with the cannibal. I have visited the islands of the New Hebrides; I have visited the Loyalty Group; I have seen the work of missions in the Samoan Group; I have known all the islands of the Society Group; I have lived for ten years in the Hervey Group; I know a few of the groups close on the line, and for at least nine years of my life have lived with the savages of New Guinea—but I have never yet met with a single man or woman, or with a single people, that your civilisation without Christianity has civilised. For God's sake let it be done at once! Gospel and commerce, but remember this, it must be the gospel first. Wherever there has been the slightest spark of civilisation in the Southern Seas, it has been where the gospel has been preached; and wherever you find in the island of New Guinea a friendly people, or a people that will welcome you there, it is where the missionaries of the cross have been preaching Christ. Civilisation! The rampart can only be stormed by those who carry the cross."

In the report made by a Parliamentary Committee in 1837, of which Mr. Gladstone is the only survivor, the following strong language is used:—
" It is not too much to say that the intercourse of Europeans in general, without any exception in favour of the subjects of Great Britain, has been, unless when attended by missionary exertions, a source of many calamities to uncivilised nations."

It is an interesting fact that in similar reports made by the United States Government, concerning the condition of the Red Indian tribes, a similar assertion is made : " When the Government wholly failed, the voluntary efforts of the Churches have been crowned with success. The preaching of the gospel has done the work, and it alone." [1]

Instead of merely answering criticisms based on ignorance of the facts, let the following statement suffice regarding the results which can be proved almost invariably to follow from the contact of higher with lower races. In the first place, this contact, as it becomes more and more intimate, and as education and the reading of foreign literature spreads, tends to destroy the faiths of these peoples in their own religions. Now, every religion has been a centre of strength for preserving some measure of order and decency in the social life of the humblest peoples. The richer the faith, the stronger has been its influence in this regard, the higher the sanction which it seems to afford to the ideas of rectitude obtaining among the people. Naturally, therefore, the removing of faith introduces disorder into the social life, and tends to lower the character of the individuals so affected. The evidence for this is especially abundant from among the higher races. The Marquis Ito, one of Japan's greatest statesmen, who has done so much

[1] *Linguistic and Oriental Essays*, 3rd Series. By R. N. Cust, LL.D., pp. 359, 362. For a terrible description of the effects upon lower races of unchristian civilisation, *vide ibid.*, 2nd Series, pp. 533, 536.

to bring in the new Japan of to-day, though not a
Christian himself, has recently said that he and
his associates have always looked with favour upon
missions, and they are now certain that the presence
of Christians in the land saved the students, even
in the Government schools, from sinking into
an immediate immorality which would otherwise
have been unavoidable.   That is to say, this man,
who is an authority regarding Japan's attempted
rush into civilisation, says that this rush was
accompanied by a terrible dissolution of such
sanctions as had hitherto obtained among the
youth of the land.   And he sees that a widespread
immorality would have been the result.   The same
experience has presented, on a vaster scale, terrific
problems to the rulers of India.   It was one of the
earliest observations of Dr. Duff, as well as of
Christian men amongst those who were in positions
of civil authority in that Empire, that the young
men who attended the Government schools, having
lost all faith in their own gods, showed marked
tendencies towards unscrupulous and licentious
modes of life.

The second effect which is produced by this
contact of culture with heathen forms of civilisation is, that the native forms of government cease
to be effective.   This appears especially in cases
like those of the South African tribes; but one of
the most notorious and remarkable is that of
Hawaii, whose governmental history has been so
full of incident and change in recent years.   When
a number of Europeans have settled within their

10

territory, and have begun to affect the tribal life and habits by means of trade, the chiefs begin to find their hold upon their own people loosened. The Europeans, being most evidently superior to all the natives, and even to their chiefs, and being sometimes apt to treat the latter with freedom and an air of condescension, do undoubtedly help to bring the chiefs into contempt among their own subjects. One can easily see that, as Europeans settle in increasing numbers among such peoples, their evident power gradually overshadows the authority of those who hitherto have been the guardians of law and order in those regions, and oftentimes great disorder ensues. Here again the natural tendency of civilisation, as such, is not to elevate the lower races.

Not so is it that the Christian religion acts in such cases. For if it be true that war and trade and secular education have not tended to civilise but to destroy heathen peoples, it is nevertheless evidently true that scores of races have not only been saved from extinction, but have been placed in what seems to be the line of continuous progress by the work of the missionaries.

This is a fact of such extraordinary importance for our understanding of the progress of man that we ought to look somewhat closely into it. By what means is it that the religion of Christ, as taught by the missionary, has produced the momentous effects here alleged? We have already glanced at this matter in connection with the spread of education. But we must in this place go a little deeper into the substance of the problem. In the first place, the gospel of Christ, while it humbles all those who enter into its teaching and receive its spirit, yet confers upon them a new self-respect. To a man who has considered himself little more than the mere slave of a chief, or has lived in utter ignorance of his destiny, sleeping, hunting, and eating, the changes wrought by the inflow of Christian faith have the force of a revolution. What must it mean to such a man to receive the inward consciousness of what Christians call eternal life, of sonship towards God? And what must it mean to him to see and feel the brotherhood that connects him with the white missionary and all whom he represents? He stands now in a new world, in relations to God which awaken in him the hope of a new and glorious destiny, in relations to man which awaken a new sense of humanity. This naturally creates a nobler spirit. As a larger outlook, thus gained, dignifies all the personal habits and ways of every man so affected, the action of the gospel through them upon the social civilisation must be very evident. A sense of decency is awakened with that new consciousness, and desire for ampler surroundings in what the native begins to call his home; his ideas of comfort become refined; his whole life rapidly assumes something of the aspects of civilisation.

This point has been well illustrated by Dr. Lindley, a well-known missionary among the Zulus. "The first evidence of coming to Christ among the Zulus was the sense of comparative nakedness. A man, for instance, goes to mission premises, and for some small article which he barters in trade obtains a common calico shirt, worth from fivepence to sixpence. Then, putting that on, he comes the next day for a pair of common duck pants, costing about the same amount. He cannot have comfort of that shirt without something to cover his nether extremities. Then the next day he goes back, and he wants a three-legged stool, such as those on which, when we were boys, perhaps we used to milk the cows; for he must not sit on the ground any more and soil his pants. Now, when that man gets that calico shirt and those duck pants on, and he sits on that stool nine inches high, he is about nine thousand miles above all the heathen round about him." [1]

Not only so, the Spirit of Christ has been said from the beginning to act directly upon moral character; and illustrations literally teem throughout all missionary reports, from all parts of the world, regarding the immediate transformation of character, which begins as soon as the sway of Christ is acknowledged by the conscience and affections of even the most degraded man. Most thrilling, for example, is the story of the Canadian Indian whose heart burned within him to avenge the murder of his son by a trusted companion. He heard a missionary preach on the words of Jesus: "Father, forgive them, for they know not

[1] *L. M. C.*, vol. i., p. 182.

what they do." The gospel had taken hold of his heart, and when he heard the direct application of this passage made to himself,—" if you would be a Christian, you must be Christlike. He forgave and prayed for His murderers; and to be like Him, you must forgive even the man who has done you the greatest harm,"—the lesson went home. The chief actually had the manhood and the courage to say, when the opportunity for vengeance came and the murderer was in his power, " As I wish Christ to forgive me, so I forgive you." Who can measure the cost of that action to that man ? It was a great sacrifice when he threw away that opportunity, for that reason, and thus broke with the traditions of his tribe, with the habits of his own lifetime, quelled the turbulent impulses of his heart, and introduced not only into his own conduct, but into the life of the tribe, this vision of a higher and nobler spirit. It is indeed by sacrifices like this, by countless acts of self-control and self-conquest, that morality spreads and civilisation of the higher type becomes possible. We are told that never again did this man go on the war-path ; and from that one fact we see how, for him, one act of renunciation in regard to one sinful practice flooded with light whole tracts of tribal customs which hitherto had seemed both right and natural. So, again, is it that the Christian religion has ever tended rapidly to carry men past the lower stages of progress, for it has blotted out by a clear and awful revelation entire classes of evil traditions and degrading habits.

Or from another region let us take another example. Mr. J. G. Paton, lonely and sick in the island of Tanna, can only depend upon the assistance of two people, a man and his wife, who had not long before this practised cannibalism. Yet of the man he writes: "Any trust, however sacred or valuable, could be absolutely reposed in him; and in trial or danger I was often refreshed by that old teacher's prayers, as I used to be by the prayers of my saintly father in my childhood's home. No white man could have been a more valuable helper to me in my perilous circumstances, and no person, white or black, could have shown more fearless and chivalrous devotion." [1]

Again, take an example from yet another portion of the missionary field. A certain reformer in Japan was foully assassinated. He had a relative who became a Christian, and ultimately a native pastor. Many years after the death of his brother, he was celebrating the Lord's Supper, when an old man got up and said: "I am one of those who wounded that man twenty-five years ago, and I confess my share in the crime." The reply of the pastor was: "By all the ancient customs of Japan I am bound to avenge that blood-feud by plunging my dagger into the throat of the man who was the murderer of my relative; but Christ's blood reconciles all blood-feuds, and in Christ's name I wish to extend to this brother the right hand of fellowship." [2]

Not only do missionaries see and therefore

[1] *J. G. Paton*, p. 173.

[2] *Japan: Its People and Missions*, by Jessie Page, p. 72.

believe in the remarkable ethical changes wrought by the power of their religion; the natives themselves are quick to mark the facts. A story, for example, is told of a bank officer in Japan, who came to the missionary in utter despair over the fact that the young Japanese who were employed in a national bank were proving themselves utterly untrustworthy. They were very clever at their work, and made excellent cashiers, tellers, book-keepers, and clerks; but they were thoroughly dishonest, and those who were in authority could see no way of raising up a race of honest bank clerks. This bank officer admitted that he did not believe in any religion whatsoever. He claimed that the Japanese intellect was of too philosophical a nature to accept the Jewish myth called Christianity. " But," he said, " your religion does something that our religion cannot do; it makes men honest. Now we wish our employés to be carefully instructed in these principles, so that they may discharge their duties with integrity." [1]

Dr. Post, the great medical missionary of Syria, narrates the following interesting incident.[2] Many years ago a governor - general in Syria dismissed his staff of native physicians for incompetency and corruption. He applied at the College at Beirut for a corps of its graduates, and, in doing so, he said : " It is not merely because of their superior scientific

---

[1] Dr. Maclay's *A Budget of Letters from Japan*, p. 216 ; quoted by Rev. John Liggins, in *The Great Value and Success of Foreign Missions*.

[2] In *Missions at Home and Abroad*, p. 846.

attainments, but because I have confidence in their moral character, that I choose my staff from them."

The work of the missionary, when he acts as an agent of civilisation, depends for method upon the kind and degree of civilisation which he finds in the scene of his labours. For example, when the early missionaries first began work in the cannibal islands of the South Seas, amongst people who were extremely ignorant, as well as extremely savage, whose social life possessed only the rudiments of organisation, their work as civilisers would be quite direct and open. They not only had to instil the elements of religious faith into the minds of the natives, but begin immediately thereafter to teach them the simpler arts. Those whom they employed as servants and helpers in building their houses, making their own furniture, tilling their own gardens, became teachers of others. Examples of this literally abound in every direction. The following passage is typical. It describes the state of matters which Bishop Selwyn found in a certain part of New Zealand on his first tour of inspection. "Nor was it religion only which had been taught to this promising race; agriculture also and the arts of civilised life had long ago been introduced. So long ago as 1830, the station at Waimate had made itself independent of New South Wales for its supplies of provisions. More than fifty thousand bricks were made; seven hundred thousand feet of timber were felled; three wooden houses were erected, with stabling for twelve or fourteen horses; eight or ten cottages were built, and, ultimately, a spacious chapel, ploughs, and harrows were constructed; and roads were cut through the dense forests; while January 3, 1835, was made for ever memorable by the introduction of a printing-press, to be worked by a native assistant." Can we wonder that Charles Darwin wrote of this field: " I took leave of the New Zealand missionaries with feelings of high respect for their useful and upright characters. . . . The march of improvement, consequent on the introduction of Christianity throughout the South Seas, probably stands by itself in the record of history."[1]

The missionary has often been in a position to advise both the chiefs and the people as to many matters connected with the tribal life. Their evil customs he has openly rebuked, their cruelties and ignorance and lawlessness he has sought to remove by the establishment of some rational system of legislation and administration.

One only needs to read narratives of the work done in Hawaii, in Fiji, and in New Guinea, to see that in such cases the missionary has acted almost as a chief whose moral authority and influence was practically supreme in the tribe. It is one of the sublime spectacles of this century, one of the most remarkable signs of progress within the Christian Church itself, that in all such cases Protestant missionaries have consistently striven to establish the power of others; they have not even been tempted to assume the reins of power, when such a step would have been attended with no danger

[1] *Life of G. A. Selwyn*, by Canon Curteis, pp. 69, 70.

or difficulty, and would have seemed even to the leaders of the church in earlier ages to give to the cause of Christianity a great opportunity of obtaining sway amongst the natives. The missionaries, I say, have without exception avoided a step which the whole church now sees would have proved disastrous to the truest interests of the gospel. So much, at anyrate, has been learned from the experience of Europe regarding the relations of church and state.

When we go amongst people who are found in a somewhat better condition as to organisation and habits of life, as, for example, many of the tribes in South Africa and the remarkable Hova tribe of Madagascar, we find that the influence of the missionary, though obvious and powerful, is yet exercised less directly than in the former cases. Here the advice given and personal influence exerted are more private and personal, though conferences of a more or less formal nature with the chief or king and his representatives upon public affairs may sometimes take place. Here also the presence of the missionary has resulted in the moulding of the tribal character and policy in many and most remarkable ways. In fact, as regards Madagascar, it may be said that the extraordinary strides which were taken during the last thirty years towards civilised methods of government and improved moral conditions, were the direct outcome of the counsel and guidance given at many critical points to the king or queen, and his or her advisers, by the heralds of the Christian religion.

When we come to observe the influence of missions upon civilisation in the ancient empires of the East, we find a different state of matters. In Japan and India and China the missionary enters into the midst of civilisation, possessed of dignified and ancient histories. He cannot approach rulers and administrators with the same simplicity and directness as among the simpler tribes to which we have already referred. Here everything is more imposing, more elaborate, more formal. Conservatism of the most unyielding kind has settled its dark shadows over the land. Moreover, ancient and native religions have saturated the whole system of life with their influence. The worship of gods, the observance of religious ceremonials, are bound up with almost every act of daily life and with every institution in society. The attempts of the missionary to procure reformations where customs are most cruel or most abominable are just as hopeless in those lands as if an obscure minister from an obscure village were to walk into the House of Congress at Washington, or the House of Commons in London, and demand a change in the vital policy of the American or British Government. And yet it remains to be said, that in these very lands the missionary forces are exerting an almost incalculable influence. Many of the leading rulers of great Indian provinces have borne witness to the fact that the missionaries' influence has done most to secure the remarkable changes which have taken place in regard to many Indian customs and religious observances. The old East India Company government lived in such dread of rebellions, that they weakly tolerated, and even at last shamefully participated in, some of the worst of these customs And early in the missionary movement, that which they feared most was, lest the missionaries should seek to interfere with what they considered funda- mental native institutions. Nevertheless, the missionaries speedily gave voice to their judgment on these things. Henry Martyn and William Carey burned in heart over the sufferings and the shame imposed continually upon thousands of their fellow-beings in India by these fearful heathen institutions. And when the time came, when the missionary influence had grown powerful enough, and when, above all, amongst the rulers themselves there began to appear men of noble Christian character and lofty ideals, the work of moralising this ancient civilisation began. Some of the results have been summed up in the following striking manner by Canon Hole :—

"Seventy years ago (I quote from a statement published in India, in the *Indian Watchman*) the fires of Suttee were publicly blazing in the Presi- dency towns of Madras, Bombay, and Calcutta, and all over India; the fires of Suttee, in which the screaming and struggling widow, in many cases herself a mere child, was bound to the body of her husband, and with him burned to ashes. Seventy years ago young infants were publicly thrown into the Ganges, as sacrifices to the god of the river. Seventy years ago young men and maidens, decked with flowers, were slain in Hindu temples before the hideous idol of the goddess Kali, or hacked to pieces at the Meras, that their quivering flesh might be given to propitiate the god of the soil. Seventy years ago the cars of Juggernaut were rolling over India, crushing hundreds of human victims annually-beneath their wheels. Seventy years ago lepers were burned alive, devotees publicly starved themselves to death, children brought their parents to the bank of the Ganges, and hastened their death by filling their mouths with the sand and the water of the so-called sacred river. Seventy years ago the swinging festival attracted thousands to see the poor writhing wretches, with iron hooks thrust through the muscles of their backs, swinging in mid-air in honour of their gods. For these scenes, which disgraced India seventy years ago, we may now look in vain. And need I remind you that every one of these changes for the better is due directly or indirectly to missionary enterprise, and the spirit of Christianity? It was Christian missionaries, and those who supported them, who proclaimed and denounced these tremendous evils. Branded as fanatics, and satirised as fools, they ceased not until one by one these hideous hallucinations were suppressed." [1]

To turn to Japan again for one moment, we find that even the Japanese recognise the great influence exerted by the Christian religion upon the extraordinary developments which have taken place

[1] Quoted in *The Great Value and Success of Foreign Missions*, by Rev. J. Liggins, pp. 90, 91.

in that country during the last century. A leading citizen of Tokyo said in an address, that the
younger men did not know what older Japan was,
and that practically the Christian missionaries had
" saved the Empire." One of the leading missionaries of that land (Mr. S. L. Gulick) has said:
" The Kingdom of God is coming in Japan as in
no other non-Christian land. The national ideas
as to government, education, morality, justice,
law, and the family have become in fact largely
Christian."

The difficulties of direct influence are, of course,
greater in China than in any other land; for there
the Government remains stolidly indifferent and
separate from missions. The missionaries are
looked down upon as of the poor and the despised
classes. It is only through slow processes, especially perhaps through the translated Bible and
medical missionaries, that access is being obtained
to the higher classes of Chinese society. It is too
early yet to say in what direction that ancient civilisation will be moulded by the evangelical spirit.
It is evident that in all such cases the missionary
can only modify the conditions of civilisation,
through the Christian literature which is in circulation and through the work of teaching and influ-
encing one individual after another. Of course,
through the Christian literature, he can secure the
presentation of the ideals of the Christian spirit to
a very large and ever-increasing circle of readers.
The subtle influence of truth, when she shines with
her own peerless light on the dark customs of

heathendom, it is beyond our power to indicate or tabulate. We may say this much, however, that wherever the Christian religion is being learned from her own literatures, there the intrinsic reality and beauty of her ideals will begin to affect the heart and imagination, the mind and the conscience of every heathen reader. Of course, the most powerful civilising influence which in such lands the missionary exercises, is through the direct moulding of the character of individuals. Wherever Christian churches are formed under faithful oversight, and the members manifest even some lineaments of the character of Christ, surrounding society cannot possibly remain unaffected. The natural conscience of man is aroused to sensitiveness, when neighbours manifest the chief characteristics of an ideal man.

One fact is of great importance. While the evidence for it is drawn from India primarily, one can, after the experience of Europe during these eighteen hundred years, prophesy with great confidence that the same phenomena will appear in China and Japan. In India there are vast portions of population consisting of poor, and, as we say, of primitive peoples. They have practically no education, they are of no caste, or of very low caste. They are not the people to whom a Government would look hopefully, or from whom aristocratic Brahmins would expect much. But, if all signs fail not, the redemption of India may be reached through these people. For already not only have many hill-tribes received the Christian religion and entered upon careers of great promise, but the inhabitants of the vast plains in South Central India show the same eagerness to receive the gospel, and the gospel is manifesting its ancient ennobling and civilising power amongst them. The missionaries complain bitterly that they have not money wherewith to pay for the teachers and evangelists who are demanded by these peoples. Sometimes a whole village is ready to cast away its idols, turn its temple into a school, receive a Christian teacher, and avow the discipleship of Jesus Christ. The missionaries have actually to restrain their ardour with·sad hearts, for lack of funds. But they turn their eyes with brighter thoughts to the villages where already work has been begun ; for there they see the abundant signs of a transformation of character and life which is so surprising that the members of the higher castes are filled with astonishment and even with envy at the changes which are visible. These people have a new look, the cringing fear of their social superiors has disappeared ; nor has it given place to insolence, but to the dignity of that self-respect which Christianity bestows. They become industrious, intelligent, and full of enterprise. They build better houses, do better work, make more money. Some of them become teachers and preachers. In fact, the lowest classes of India have received that impulse which will carry them to the top of the social scale, and it comes from their faith in Christ and their new spiritual experience.

One of the elements which must be considered

in estimating the influence of the missionary is the impression universally made by his personal character. The natives throughout the world very speedily learn to distrust the average European trader and traveller.[1] But as steadily as this revelation of character is made, the trustworthiness of the missionary becomes more and more apparent.[2] His word can be depended upon; his kindness is untiring; his fairness in matters of dispute is unquestioned; his own unselfishness in matters of business and where money is concerned, after the first suspicions have passed away, becomes visible to all, and a matter of public observation and wonder. Alike among the older civilisations of

[1] Sir William Hunter, the distinguished Indian Administrator, says: "The confidence of the people of India in the purity and unselfishness of the motives of the missionaries is complete, and neither the officials nor any other class of foreign residents is held in so much esteem as they are."

[2] Another instance of the same trust which the missionaries awaken in the hearts of heathen people is to be found in the strange act of a South African chief, Sekhome by name. He had for long been stirring up strife amongst his people, seeking to drive out the missionary, persecuting his own sons who were earnest Christians, and had even created a civil war by attacking the latter and the Christian party who sympathised with them. Yet, when all his vile machinations had failed, and he himself become a fugitive, fearing vengeance, it was to the missionary he fled. On that evening when he left his own royal courtyard and fled to the rocks and the caves, "a solitary figure," we are told by the missionary, "was observed descending the mountain near to my house. It was Sekhome. He could no longer trust his own people; he knew that he could still trust the missionary. He seemed relieved when he entered the house. I had now a glorious opportunity of rewarding good for evil, and took advantage of it." (*Ten Years North of the Orange River*, by John Mackenzie, pp. 449 ff.).

11

the East and the poor tribes of Africa or the South Seas this faith in the missionary is a fact notorious and indisputable. He lives what his religion teaches. On the whole, he is seen to manifest the outlines of the character of Jesus Christ, and this gives an enormous power to his teaching and his exhortations.

Yet another, and perhaps the steadiest and most powerful of all single instruments of civilisation that can be named is the missionary home. The home life is the fountain-head of the character of a people. The relations that exist there give character and form to all other relations in the social system. Where mutual trust and love and honour exist among the members of the homes of a people, these qualities will inevitably stream out, like light from a centre of light, upon the surrounding system. It is the evidence of one who has had unsurpassed opportunity of observation in different parts of the world, "that one Christian missionary home, with a Christian wife, does more to humanise, elevate, and evangelise a race of people than twenty celibate men." [1] It is a perception of this fact that led, for example, a Japanese missionary (Rev. C. A. Clark) to open his house, invite visitors from the surrounding country, and show them the whole of the interior arrangements, in parlour and kitchen ; explain to them the uses of the children's room, the stoves and the wire mattress, which were chief curiosities; explain to them also the reasons for the absence of the god-

[1] Rev. Wardlaw Thompson, *L. M. C.*, vol. i., p. 409.

shelf, which they immediately missed. In two years this missionary received into his home no fewer than 12,000 visitors. He made his house the centre of a lending library and reading-room. All this was done with the simple purpose of giving the Japanese an opportunity for seeing and feeling something of the characteristics of a Christian home. How much, even in Japan, this special influence is needed, may be gathered from such facts as the following:—The Japanese home is said to consist of "father, mother, concubines, and various sorts of children, who are born of the wife or of the concubines, or have been adopted into the family. Filial piety, which no doubt exists and is insisted upon, is distorted into a horrible outrage upon humanity, and especially on womanhood. The father may always command the daughter to sell herself into a life of shame to pay his debts, and she incurs merit by this act of sacrifice." [1]

In China, where annually no fewer than two hundred thousand infants are put to death, the influence of Christianity on the home life is transforming many of the conditions which form the worst features of the Chinese civilisation. Chinese Christian homes are verily fountains of most blessed influence upon the community. A well-known lady missionary from China has said: "The women in these Christian homes become true, devoted, and earnest Christians. . . . It is a blessed thing to go into one of these homes, where there is a Christian mother, and see the stimulating in-

[1] *The Religions of Japan*, by W. E. Griffis, D.D., pp. 122, 123.

fluence which she exerts, compared to the misery of the home where the heathen mother exerts her influence."[1]

In India the same momentous results are following the exertions which are being made by all missionary societies to establish and extend Zenana work. Leading Indians see the significance of this. They feel that through the home the missionary is conquering India. And yet, because the women medical missionaries bring their skill to bear upon the suffering and disease of the women in their homes, they are unwilling to shut the door against them. Some of the more far-sighted of the educated Hindus have openly acknowledged that through their influence upon the home life these Christian missionaries have at last captured the stronghold of the ancient Indian faiths and civilisation. Travellers, like Miss Gordon Cumming, who have gone to the South Seas, and watched the manner of life of the natives in islands, like Fiji, which have been most profoundly affected by Christianity, express their amazement at the transformation of the home life. The houses have more than one room; the father and mother are faithful to one another, train their children in the Christian faith, maintain daily family worship, filling the villages at eventide with songs of praise. And these people were, many of them, cannibals not many years ago.[2]

The consideration of the influence exerted by

[1] Mrs. Edge, *L. M. C.*, vol. i., p. 114.
[2] Cf. *At Home in Fiji*, by C. F. Gordon Cumming.

the missionary home upon native peoples inevitably suggests a subject to which I can only briefly refer, but one which for the future of the race is of immeasurable importance; I mean the status of woman. In no heathen land does woman receive a modicum of the respect and honour which we see to be her rightful due. The degradation of womankind is one of the darkest accompaniments of heathenism, and one of the strongest barriers against the progress of the race. The elevation of the home life means, first and last, the elevation of woman. As she receives her due place in the thought and affection of her husband and sons and brothers, her own nature is ennobled; the deeper and finer instincts of her soul are awakened to dominate her life; she becomes the gracious and purifying influence which Christianity has made her, and Christendom now finds her to be.

We have seen in this chapter the chief methods by which the religion of Christ is moulding the civilisation of the heathen world. We have seen that when the individual becomes converted, he comes under influences which begin more or less rapidly to change his personal habits of thought and life. The lower the past life of such a man, the more striking are the results immediately following his conversion. We have seen that the work of enlightening, guiding, strengthening that man is carried on by means of the church and its adjunct, the school. We have also seen that as soon as a few people have been gathered together, family life assumes a higher and purer tone, and from that centre very strong influences flow out upon the surrounding community. *The great work of civilising the world is thus effected by the Church of Christ through the moralising of the individual and the family.* In the simpler tribes the immediate effect is to create new personal and social wants which are closely allied with the maintenance of decency and comfort. Amid the more elaborate institutions of India, the first civil effect of Christianity has been seen in the removal of various customs which seemed to be deeply rooted in the national life, but which were with comparative ease eliminated as soon as the light of a higher conscience shone upon them and condemned them. The further modification of the social conditions in those Eastern lands must necessarily be a somewhat slow process. But there can be little doubt that each decade will mark a steady progress, and that the most potent force will prove to be the rapidly increasing Christian community with its keener conscience and its loftier ideals.

CHAPTER VIII

THE MISSIONARY AND OTHER RELIGIONS

It is now recognised, practically by all investigators and thinkers, that religion is universal. No tribe can be found which does not possess a religion of some kind. This means that it belongs to human nature, both as we know it now and so far as history can discover its past operations, to be conscious of some kind of connection with that which is called the superhuman or supernatural. This implies, of course, that there must always be some point of connection which can be found between the crudest forms of belief and Christianity. Were it not for this, Christian missions would be impossible. If the preacher of Jesus Christ could not find some instinct, some working of conscience, some apprehension of the mind, some movement of the imagination, even amongst the lowest races, which manifests an affinity with the highest attainments of Christian experience, he could not begin his work. But this just means that if a race so utterly destitute could be discovered, it would be one that is for ever entirely cut off from the rest of mankind. No elevation of

167

such a people could possibly take place in any direction. The very absence of the possibility of a religion would relegate them to a separate species. " These ideas," said J. G. Paton of the New Hebrides, concerning his work amongst the cannibals, " had to be woven into their spiritual consciousness, had to become the very warp and woof of their religion. But it could be done,—that we believed,—because they were men, not beasts." [1]

We know now far more fully than in any earlier generation the characteristics of the various religions throughout the world. The poorest form of fetishism has been subjected, and is being subjected, to close scientific scrutiny by men of the highest scholarship and ability ; and, needless to say, the elaborate and higher religions of the East are exercising a wonderful fascination upon the minds of scholars and thinkers. In this work of investigating the actual forms of belief possessed by the natives, the grounds of those beliefs and their effects upon the morals and civilisation of the people who hold them, the missionaries are, as a class, supremely interested and ceaselessly diligent. It is true that we every now and again hear a piece of condescending advice, from one direction or another, suggesting that the missionaries *should* study the religions of the people to whom they preach, and *should* try to employ whatever is of value in those religions, making these points of contact the starting-points for higher instruction. But there surely have been few missionaries, and

[1] *J. G. Paton*, p. 121.

they both foolish in mind and futile in labour, who have ever needed such advice. It may have been held by a few people in the early history of the missionary movement, say three-quarters of a century ago, that the light of Christianity is self-evident, that the missionary needs only to let it shine through his declarations to allow him the joy of seeing multitudes arise and accept it. But those who held this view in ignorance must have speedily found it impossible. Since the day when Henry Martyn thought that a miracle was necessary ere a Hindu could be converted, all intelligent supporters of missions, and all missionaries themselves, have realised that their relation to the religions of the heathen world is much more intricate and intimate than that picture would suggest. As Sir William Hunter has said: "We no longer suppose it possible for an ignorant and zealous man to go forth, simply armed by his own desire to do what is right and state the truth; we no longer believe it possible for that man to succeed." [1]

It may not be too bold to say that probably the missionaries, more than any other class of men, rejoice over every feature of value which they can discover in heathen religions.[2] For every element

[1] *L. M. C.*, vol. i., p. 14.

[2] "Though the missionary has resources which the physician has not, still it cannot but help him if he starts with a knowledge of the savage's point of view. To the necessity of such knowledge for the missionary, no more eloquent testimony could be given than is afforded by the labour which missionaries have bestowed on the study of native religions, and which provides most of the material for the history of early forms of religion."—*Introduction to the History of Religion*, by F. B. Jevons, p. 6.

of truth which these contain, every form of sensitiveness to the higher ethical demands and religious affirmations of Christianity which they reveal, makes it easier for the missionary to approach the people, makes him more hopeful of seeing his own great message take hold and do its work. It is a well-known missionary of the East who said: "These delicious glimmerings of light we do find by patient search in the religions of the Orient, and in the existence of such we missionaries who have to combat those systems continually rejoice. We gladly use those flashes of light in bringing home the truth to the people, as did Paul at Athens. . . . But we sadly recognise how utterly inadequate is that light to lead sinful man to peace with God."[1]

The missionary believes, with the whole Christian church, that all these religions are about to be displaced by the Christian faith. He does not wish to see them merely destroyed; for the mere destruction of these religions, without the supply of what is more adequate, would be only deplorable. That which is hoped for and is being worked for with such infinite ardour, self-sacrifice, and hope is the substitution of the Christian religion for all other forms of religion whatsoever. The missionary longs for the day when there shall be placed before all men the one severe and inevitable alternative between Christianity and an irreligious life. Then it will not be possible for a man to think it worth while proving that he has any other positive relation

[1] Rev. Dr. Chamberlain, *The Religions of the Orient*, p. 10.

to the Unseen and the Eternal than that which is revealed and granted in the gospel of Jesus Christ.

So far as the work of evangelising the world has gone, various effects have been produced in relation to the other religions of the world. In the first place, and as might be expected, the lower forms of religion wholly and rapidly disappear. All those which have a poor intellectual groundwork, which have had less of the ideal in them, and which have had less connection with the ethical life, give way at once, like children's sandheaps when the rising tide washes over them. The earlier missionaries in the South Sea Islands were not only rejoiced, but utterly amazed, to discover with what ease whole tribes could sometimes be persuaded of the absurdity of their idolatrous beliefs. On several occasions, when the missionaries sent native evangelists in advance of them, they arrived some months afterwards to find that the revolt against idolatry had taken place merely by the teaching and arguments of those evangelists. It was a comparatively simple matter in some of these cases to prove that the idols most dreaded had no power, and to persuade the leaders of the tribe to have done with a religion based on such worthless conceptions.

It is when we come to consider the relation of Christianity to the great religions of the East that the problem assumes some complexity, and the discussion possesses great importance. Nowhere are the difficulties of this contact between Christianity and its rivals more widely felt, more carefully weighed, than in India. For, as has been said, "it is the peculiar distinction of India that it has been the theatre of nearly all the religions." There we have at anyrate those two great religions, Hinduism, with the elements of Buddhism which it contains, and Mohammedanism; while in Ceylon we have an intelligent and aggressive Buddhism. These religions, like Christianity, profess to be founded, first, upon historical revelation, and, second, upon philosophical conceptions. Each of them is able to point to events in the distant past through which they assert that the supreme truth regarding man and his spiritual relations was made known. And they are able, in support of the reality, nature, and results of this revelation, to adduce what they consider more or less irrefragable metaphysical principles. These facts make the task of conviction very much more difficult. And the question which many persons are inclined to ask is, whether there is hope that these religions will be speedily displaced by the Christian faith. This half-sceptical wonder has in recent years been very considerably increased by the attempts that have been made in Europe and America to rehabilitate some of these Oriental religions. Oriental enthusiasts, theosophists, and spiritualistic cranks, have combined, by means of their imagery and mysticism and their ethical enthusiasm, to suffuse over the greatest Asiatic religions a glory which is not their own. Constant appeal is made to the facts that, in a sense, many of these are older than the Christian religion, have secured dominance over the minds of hundreds of millions of the human race,[1] and contain in their sacred writings a very large number of noble and inspiring ethical principles and exhortations.

Let us ask ourselves regarding the fitness of these religions to cope with Christianity in meeting and satisfying the deepest needs of men ?

And, first, looking at the matter from the purely *religious* point of view, the following statements seem to me to be within the mark, and easily defensible. Christianity is infinitely superior to Buddhism in that the latter is practically atheistic or agnostic, while the gospel of Christ finds its fountain - head in the doctrine of a living and personal God. No people have been long content with a mere negation regarding the ultimate Being or Fact which is the ground of all life, and, there-fore, the object of all hope. Hence we find that, in those regions where Buddhistic teaching has exercised its influence, the general masses of the people have not been content with Buddha's own placid nescience regarding God.[2] The heart of man reaches out into the unseen, feeling after that which is personal, and, judged from the purely religious point of view, that religion would seem

[1] The number of Buddhists has been often greatly exaggerated. "The best authorities are of the opinion that there are not more than one hundred millions of real Buddhists in the world."— *Buddhism*, by Sir M. Monier-Williams, p. 15.

[2] "As it (Buddhism) is atheistic in its origin, it very soon becomes infected by the most fantastic mythology and the most childish superstitions" (Art. "Religions," in *Encyclop. Brit.*, by C. P. Tiele).

to be the highest, the last in the order of evolution, and the fittest to control the homage of mankind, which contains the deepest and most illuminative affirmations concerning a supreme and personal God.

As one student has well said of the Buddhist religion: "Its ideal is to empty life of everything active and positive, rather than to concentrate energy on a strong purpose. It does not train the affections to virtuous and harmonious action, but denies to them all action and consigns them to extinction. This condemnation it has incurred by parting with that highest stimulus to human virtue and endeavour, which lies in the belief in a living God."[1] The pessimism of Buddha is not a feature which is made prominent by the people who recommend Buddhism to our Western world. But it was central to the teaching and spirit of Buddha himself. For him conscious existence was an evil so dire and painful that he believed religion consisted in the prolonged effort to escape from it. This could be accomplished, he thought, by a gradual separation of self from all passion, from all self-exaltation, from all, in fact, that would nourish the desire for personal existence. Hence the need of winning the heart from all lusts of the flesh, and preserving a mind that is meek and lowly. The end thereof is not life, but the loss of life. For that purpose seek pureness, ensure those rare virtues,—simply in order the more certainly and speedily to cease to be. That is the soul of

[1] *History of Religion*, by Professor Menzies, D.D., p. 379.

Buddhism, its strongest motive and its loftiest
ambition. Christianity will displace Buddhism,
because the latter is a religion "having no hope,
and without God in the world."

Then, in the next place, Christianity is superior
to Mohammedanism, because of the relations which
it establishes between the worshipper and the
living God. Mohammedanism, though it arose
after Christianity, and owes some of its most
powerful features to Mohammed's vague acquaintance with the Jewish and Christian religions, yet
belongs in order of religious value to an earlier
stage of development. It is strikingly and severely
monotheistic; but its God is one whose ethical
qualities are ill defined, whose personal relations
to the worshipper do not invite responsive faith,
love, and service. The worshipper feels a reverence
for Allah, but at a great distance. He believes in
the protection of Allah, but it is the protection
of merely physical force against foes. As to the
inward life of worship, and overshadowing of the
wings of an infinite and watchful love, which is
characteristic of Christianity, Mohammedanism
knows nothing.

Yet again, Christianity is superior to the vast
and subtle religion of Hinduism. This can be
proved thoroughly only by comparing the one
religion with the other, point by point.[1] Suffice it
here to make one general comparison. Hinduism is
proud of being what it would call universal. It

[1] Cf. *Buddhism*, by Sir M. Monier-Williams, Lect. xviii. Also
F. F. Ellinwood, D.D., in *L. M. C.*, vol. i., pp. 50–60.

has succeeded in the past in absorbing into itself the teaching of one great system after another. The root of its life as an organised system is to be found in its priestcraft. It was this which transformed the earlier and simpler Nature Religion, out of which it grew, into that terrible instrument of human torture, the Brahmanism which existed in the days of Buddha. Buddhism really arose as a kind of rationalistic modification of certain aspects of this inhuman system. Over against its system of caste Buddha taught the love of man, which, whether he foresaw it or not, would tend to abolish all caste ; over against its demands for innumerable sacrifices of blood to appease angry deities, Buddha set his indifference whether there be a God or not.[1] Personal goodness seemed to him the supreme matter of interest, as over against the miserable, formal righteousness demanded by the priests. But Hinduism waited its time, and then quietly adopted Buddha himself as one of its gods, and Buddhism as a distinct religion departed from

---

[1] There has been some discussion regarding the degree of revolt against Hinduism of which Buddha may have been conscious. Some describe him as a deliberate revolutionary. Others deny that he meant to oppose any fundamental points of the older religion. His attitude seems to have had some resemblance to that of St. Francis of Assisi. In each case principles were passionately adopted whose consistent realisation would have destroyed the ecclesiasticism of the day. In each case the new preacher was met by both praise and blame, both welcome and opposition, from the authorities. In each case the purity of the new light was dimmed by being formally acknowledged and tolerated by the reigning power, and mixed up with its own lower and lowering institutions and doctrines.

India. When again Mohammedanism gained its hold on sections of the people, Hinduism adopted some of its features. And now it is striving in this century, though some think not for the first time, to take into itself those elements of Christianity which it can conveniently assimilate. There are some people who feel as if this power of indefinite assimilation seems to indicate that, in India at least, Hinduism can successfully cope with Christianity. But, on the other hand, we must remember that this system of eclecticism, the mere adoption into itself of what seems to be best in other systems, is not growth from within. It is an arbitrary proceeding. It resembles rather the enlargement of objects in the inorganic world by accretion, than the development of the energies of a living thing in the control of more and more intricate organs and their functions. Hinduism is not truly universal, because it has no true unity. It has been well called a conglomerate. Christianity, on the other hand, is universal in a true sense, in that, while it has affinities with whatever is real and valuable in all systems, it has yet a distinctive life of its own, and takes up towards all a positive and decisive attitude. While fitted for all men, it is one and the same in all men. When it recognises what is of value in Hinduism or Buddhism, it simply finds there what it already contains. Its sympathies arise not from its readiness to adopt new elements from other systems, but from the fact that the elements of good in all systems are already in its own heart.

12

Lastly, it may be pointed out that Christianity is superior to all these systems, from the purely religious point of view, in that its supreme affirmation has regard to God Himself as acting on behalf of men ; yea, as suffering with and for men. Any religion which falls short of this ideal is thereby unfitted to cope with Christianity in the effort to win the allegiance of the human heart. If we are to have any thought or image of God, any ideal of a religious relation to Him, none seems conceivable that is higher than this, that God Himself should spare not His own Son, but in view of our deep and dire need should deliver Him up for us all. Whatever is best in the pantheism of the Hindu, in the enthusiasm of the Buddhist, finds a more glorious expression and a more living energy in the gospel of Christ.

Then we must pass to a comparison of Christianity with these religions from the *social* and *ethical* point of view. It is too late merely to admit that these great religions contain many beautiful and true words regarding human relations in society. That is one of the ordinary facts known to all, which ought to make all hearts glad. Nor should any one hesitate to admit that, within certain limits, these religions have performed immense services to mankind. Concerning Buddhism Sir M. Monier-Williams has said: "It promoted progress up to a certain point. It preached purity in thought, word, and deed, though only for the storing up of merit. It proclaimed the brotherhood of humanity. It avowed sympathy with social liberty and freedom. It gave back much independence to women. It inculcated universal benevolence, extending even to animals; and from its declaration, that a man's future depended upon his present acts and conditions, it did good service for a time in preventing stagnation, promoting activity, and elevating the character of humanity." [1]

As concerning Mohammedanism, it must be said that while, where its armies have taken and conquered regions of the world which were already Christian, it has degraded their civilisation, yet, on the other hand, it has improved the social condition of some of those tribes in India and Africa whom it has overcome. It is able to raise up to its own level, but able also to drag down to its own level peoples already above it. Nevertheless in Mohammedanism, as in Buddhism and other Oriental religions, there are elements of an ethical nature, features of social teaching, which are, on the whole, of real value. Concerning the value of these elements of truth and their social influence, as compared with the moral teaching and civilising power of Christianity, two or three other facts require to be observed.

1. These true and beautiful sayings and commandments are mingled in the sacred writings of these religions with much that is wrong and even degrading. Professor Max Müller, in his introduction to the translation of the Sacred Books of the East, apologises for the fact that, though these books were being translated for scientific pur-

[1] *L. M. C*, vol. i., p. 37.

poses and the use of scholars, there were passages in them which, "though harmless and innocent in themselves, cannot be rendered in modern language without the appearance of coarseness." [1] Even though the accomplished editor suggests an explanation of this by saying that the Oriental mind regards many of these matters in a different way from us, and that man at that time "really was an animal, with all the strength and weakness of an animal," the explanation does not obliterate the fact nor minimise its significance for our argument. Upon this point Professor Chamberlain of Japan has said concerning the Kojiki, the Japanese sacred books which he translated: "The shocking obscenity of word and act to which the 'records' bear witness is another ugly feature which must not quite be passed over in silence. It is true that decency, as we understand it, is a very modern product, and it is not to be looked for in a society in a barbarous stage. At the same time, the whole range of literature might perhaps be ransacked for a parallel to the native filthiness of certain passages here." [2]

Dr. Griffis, than whom there is no higher or fairer judge of the history of religion in Japan, has said: "Buddhism has had a fair field in Japan, and its outcome has not been elevating. Its influence has been atheistic, and not ethical. It added culture and art to Japan as it brought with itself the civilisation of continental Asia." Mohammed-

[1] *The Sacred Books of the East*, vol. i., Preface, p. xxi.
[2] Quoted by W. E. Griffis, in *The Religions of Japan*, p. 66.

THE MISSIONARY AND OTHER RELIGIONS   181

anism, it must be said, suffers under the same dis-
ability as Buddhism, for the Koran also contains
much ethical teaching that is to be reprobated.

Professor Max Müller, in the passage already
referred to, describes the causes which led to the
growth of what appears to us a heterogeneous
mass of irrelevant, inferior, and oftentimes deplorable material around the purer and nobler teachings which these religions possessed. Those which
he names may be " true causes," but he omits to
mention the one condition whose absence made the
operation of these causes effective, and whose
presence saved the records of the religion of
Revelation from the same disaster. This condition
was the possession of a standard of judgment.
What standard guided the minds of the Jews in
the formation of their canon it may not be easy to
say. Assuredly it was no ideal of scientific history,
nor any modern conception of the ethics of authorship and publication. Probably the standard was
a religious one, and was derived from the prophetic
teaching about the character of Jehovah and
about His purposes and dealings with Israel. The
canonical literature of the Old Testament does on
the whole deal with these two mutually related
subjects. In the formation of the New Testament
canon the early church was guided by the ideal of
apostolic authority. The central figure in their
life and worship, the fountain-head of truth and
supreme object of intellectual interest, was, indeed,
their Saviour and Lord, Jesus Christ. But this
very fact made it the more obvious that hence-

forth the normative Christian teaching must be formed out of the writings of those who stood in unique relations to Him, both before and after His death and resurrection. This close connection between the standard of the canonical literature of the New Covenant, and the personality of Jesus, undoubtedly accounts for the unexampled freedom of the New Testament from all that is foolish and intellectually contemptible, as well as from all teaching that is unhealthy and impure.[1] The heathen religions had no such standard. The natural causes which Professor Max Müller has enumerated had freedom to act corruptingly, unintelligently upon the growth of the Sacred Books of the East.

2. Although these religions do recognise the need that men should give up certain forms of selfishness and evil doing, and live according to the higher standard, they do not provide or manifest any force that shall enable their adherents to realise this ideal. Buddhism, while urging with passion the ideals of the pure heart and the clear mind, distinctly asserts that no man can possibly escape the direct penalty of his sins. The utmost that a man can hope for is that he may be able by

---

[1] There are, indeed, in the Old Testament a few narratives of shame, and the people of Israel did pass through various stages of religious and moral attainment. It is the peculiar glory of the religion of Revelation that it has preserved the main outlines of the progress of that Revelation, and that in Jesus Christ we have the standard by means of which we can distinguish what was false or evil from what was true and good in the faith and practice of earlier days. This is the only religion in the world which possesses that feature, and no religion can be final which does not possess it.

good deeds, by pure thoughts, to lay up for himself a store of merit. How the man who is not only capable of evil, but is also sold under sin, enslaved to his past, can reform himself, has been the permanent problem of human history; and Buddhism, like Mohammedanism, has failed to provide a solution. Although in each case one man, a teacher or prophet, stands out as the founder of the religion, the revealer of all the wisdom which it contains, each of these religions suffers in comparison with Christianity, the moment one even thinks of contrasting Buddha or Mohammed with Jesus Christ. In Him the ideal man is at once the fountain of light and of strength, the object of hope and inspiration. From Him, His followers have learned; in Him they believe that they receive personal and actual invigoration; and unto Him they hope, one and all, personally to return. Were He not the Ideal Man at the beginning of their history, the hope would be no inspiration; were the hope not shining there before their eyes, the memory would be a bitter mockery; and were He only a memory and a hope, not a living presence, His followers would find it hard to pursue their ideal and to cherish their love. It is because they find in Him one who from day to day is in actual touch with their separate selves, that they have gone out to shed His light upon all parts of the earth.

3. But further, there are many positive teachings, characteristic of these religions and derived

from their founders, which we now know to have been simply blunders, and which put them, when compared with Christianity, in a realm below comparison with it. Various matters might be named in proof of this; let one be final and sufficient, as a test, *i.e.*, their teaching concerning women. As Dr. Post, that great observer and teacher, who has lived so long in Mohammedan lands, has said: "Women determine the social condition in any country and any race. No race has ever risen above the condition of its women." The condition to which Mohammedanism has reduced womankind is too well known to need description. The land of the veil is the land of woman's degradation. And this is the result of a gradual lowering of the tone of Mohammed himself. It is the result of his personal example and of the legislation which his criminal life led him to issue. His own life was the fountain from which the long-drawn-out and most wretched history of womankind in the great Mohammedan countries has been derived. And as regards Buddhism again, let this be sufficient, that Buddha had no message for womankind. As the great authority whom I have already quoted has presented it, Buddhism says: "Avoid married life; shun it as if it were a burning pit of live coals; or, having entered on it, abandon wife, children, home, and go about as celibate monks, engaging in nothing except in the meditation and recitation of Buddha's law, that is, if you aim at the highest degree of sanctification."[1] In this matter also the

[1] *Buddhism*, by Sir M. Monier-Williams, p. 562.

teaching of Buddhism appeals not merely to the words but to the example of Buddha himself. For he not only forsook his own wife and child, but encouraged others to do the same. His opening of the new religion to women was wrung from him, and did not belong to his original plan. It seems almost an impertinence to name these forms of religious teaching in the same breath with the example and precepts of Jesus Christ. Let the Christian ideal of a wife and mother and sister stand out as proof that in this matter Mohammed and Buddha are not fit even to be compared with the founder of Christianity.

The comparison of Christianity with these other religions may still further be carried out by looking at the course of their respective *historical* developments. On this matter it is sufficient to say that, while the history of Christianity has been upwards and progressive, the histories of Mohammedanism and Buddhism, not to speak of Hinduism, have been downwards. As regards the first, the lack of a true power of development is evident from the life of Mohammed himself. Concerning him Dr. Bruce of Persia has well said: " We see him in his boyhood and youth among the Arabs as a being of exceptional sincerity, truthfulness, and purity of life. From his twenty-fifth year to his fiftieth, while he is a monogamist, we see the picture of his family life; and it is perhaps one of the most beautiful that we can find in all the history of non-Christian peoples. But when we pass to his matured age and see him set up his standard in Medina as a prophet when he is fifty-two years of age, and when we study the last eleven years of his life, we are struck at once with the most awful and most terrible of contrasts."[1] Concerning Hinduism, on the other hand, it has again been well said: "The sacred books of Hinduism have degenerated from the lofty aspirations of the Vedic nature-worship to the vileness of Saktism, from the noble praises of Varuna to the low sensuality of the Tantras, from Vedic descriptions of creation, sublime as the opening of John's Gospel, to the escapades of Krishna or the polyandry which disgraced the celestial family of Pandu."[2]

No one can maintain that Mohammedanism in the Turkish Empire is a noble or pure religion, or has yielded any promise of developing into such since the early years of its military triumphs. And no one can maintain that, even in Ceylon or Japan, Buddhism has in this last century manifested any forces which are fit to carry a people forward in religious and ethical attainment. The history of these religions has been a steady decline of purity, truth, and power. On the other hand, the history of Christianity is the history of a progressive movement in thought and in personal life. The development of religious and ethical ideas in the Old Testament is now more fully described and appreciated than it has ever been before. And the

---

[1] *L. M. C.*, vol. i., p. 18. Cf. *The Life of Mahomet*, by Sir Wm. Muir, pp. 506, 507.

[2] *L. M. C.*, vol. i., p. 57.

Christian church, in spite of many dark periods that have intervened, in spite of disagreement in various directions, ecclesiastical, theological, social, and ethical, whose memory it is a pain to cherish, has yet manifested the true elements of evolution towards an ideal. Alike in the world of theology and the world of practice, the life of the Christian church can be proved to be incomparably richer, purer, nobler, and of course vaster, in the nineteenth century than in the second. Let the hymns sung in our churches, the great sermon literature, the ever-accumulating manuals of devotion to the deeper life, the wide and wise systems of charity and evangelisation, which all flow from the life of the church of Christ to-day, bear witness to the fact that it is in process of evolution toward some great ideal of worship and character, of love and purity. When you take a wide enough view of the whole course of Christian history, even after you allow for all the questionable experiments, all the miserable failures of individual men in this institution during the centuries that lie between the raising of Christ from the dead and the close of the nineteenth century, nothing can reduce the significance of this one fact, that at last one religion has been found whose life after two thousand years appears to be more vigorous and even more full of the spirit and ideal of its Founder than in any of its earlier generations.

If, then, Christianity is in process of destroying the older and most impressive systems of religion, what are the weapons by which this work is being done? On the aggressive side the weapons are twofold. In the first place, the philosophical ground-work of all these religions is being subjected to the severest test by being compelled to face the scientific and philosophical theories and achievements of the Western world. The latter are largely the creation of the Christian spirit. Generation after generation has arisen, some of whose sons in Europe and America have thought that at last the argument or the system had been discovered which would annihilate Christianity; but Christianity has triumphed over them all. And her repeated triumphs enable one, with some confidence, to say that the philosophical ground-work upon which this religion rests is incomparably the noblest and the truest which the world has yet seen. But how different is the result of that contact between Oriental religions and Occidental thought during our own generation! Concerning Buddhism, Dr. Griffis has said: "Despite its apparent interest in and harmony with statements of science, it does not hold the men of thought or those who long for the spiritual purification and elevation of Japan."[1] And in India, with some notable and remarkable exceptions, it seems to be found impossible for educated men to retain their beliefs in the religion of their fathers. The scientific and philosophical training which they receive in the higher institutions of learning makes the whole outlook of Mohammedanism and Buddhism, as these have hitherto existed, simply impossible.

[1] *The Religions of Japan*, p. 285.

Before the white light of knowledge they pale and vanish like ghosts. But in another direction scholarship is undermining the authority of these religions ; for Orientalists are investigating, with the most minute care and the most sympathetic attitude of mind, the historical origins of these religions. This process of investigation is also making it impossible for educated men to remain believers in Buddhism or Mohammedanism, as these have hitherto existed.

But this brings us to another matter of very great importance and interest. Many minds are now asking, whether or not it is possible that these Eastern religions, in the conflict with Christianity and in co-operation with it, may not give birth to a new religion which shall comprise the excellences of all religions at present in existence, exclude their errors, and so become the ideal embodiment of truth and the ideal inspiration of virtue ? The last quarter of a century has seen many most interesting experiments of this kind in the East. The action of Christianity and Western civilisation upon the adherents of these ancient religions, and upon the peoples that have been so long bound in the fetters of Hindu civilisation, has created a veritable fever of energetic independence. Men's minds are striking out in various directions, full of daring and full of hope. For example, even among Mohammedans of India there are certain men who seek to prove that the bad features of Islam, as it is historically known, such as its approval of poly-gamy, its religious devotion to war, its subjection to the authority of the Koran, are not original elements of Mohammedanism, are not essential to it, are now rather to be discarded as incidental evils that have appeared in the course of time. Some men of considerable acuteness and great earnestness are seeking in this direction to re-establish Mohammedanism, while purifying it from obvious errors. Amongst Hindus there are many who cherish strong hopes of being able to purify both Christianity and their own religion by such a process of mutual criticism. Certain of these movements have become widely known throughout Christendom. The work of Keshub Chunder Sen, in his leadership of that most interesting movement known as the Brahmo-somaj, is the best type of these. Followers of his, like Mozoomdar,[1] have done much in the spirit of their leader to throw light upon the impossibility of such a task as he undertook. Even in Japan, or rather, I should say, *of course* in Japan, where we may expect to see every kind of experiment in every line of life attempted by that sprightly people, we have various efforts at religious compromise. We are told that recently a fraternal conference was held in Tokyo, in which nineteen Buddhists, sixteen Christians, a few Shintoists, and a few others of no decidedly religious convictions, met to describe and emphasise those matters in which they agree and by virtue of which they could proceed to work amongst their fellow-countrymen. "Much was made of trying to adapt

---

[1] Cf. Mozoomdar's two most devout and interesting works, *The Oriental Christ*, and *The Spirit of God*.

Christianity to Japanese thought and character."
The Japanese periodicals described the movement as
"Yabutsu Sekken," which means, "the question of the
coming together of Buddhism and Christianity." [1]

We may expect that these experiments will be
made in still greater number and with still greater
vigour. But their success depends upon the question whether those religions contain any doctrine
or reveal any source of inspiration which is of
essential moment to the religious consciousness of
man and which Christianity does not already
contain. This is the point which many very confi-
dent prophets of the success of some such system
of eclecticism habitually forget. For, if these religions do contain some such force or truth, let it
be named, and let its absence from the Christian
church be proved. If they do not, compromise is
a logical impossibility. Yet another fact in connection with this attempt to establish a final
religion out of the ruins, as we must call them, of
the Oriental faiths is frequently ignored. When
one turns to any books or tracts intended to
describe those ethical teachings in Buddhism or
Hinduism or Mohammedanism, which are of
permanent value, we soon begin to discover that
the standard of selection is that of the spirit of
Jesus Christ. For example, when Dr. Paul Carus,
of Chicago, publishes a book of great interest and
entitles it *The Gospel of Buddha*, a brief examination reveals the fact that only a Christian man, or
a man with a Christian training, which for this

[1] *Vide* Art. by Dr. J. D. Davis, in *The Advance*, Mar. 11, 1897.

argument is the same thing, could have made this selection. And when one reads on certain of its pages that leading Buddhists in India or elsewhere have highly praised it as a summary of the essence of Buddhism, one cannot but remember that the taste of these educated people has been much moulded by their own personal acquaintance with the ethical teaching of the New Testament. After all, it seems to be the fact that all these compromises, where they are intelligently made or possess any value whatsoever, are a tribute to the incomparable truth and worth of the Christian religion. It is the Lord of the religions of the earth. They are all submitting themselves to its judgment, even in order to discover what is best in themselves and what has been most important in their own history.

One argument employed in favour of the idea that Christianity cannot cope with these great religions of India arises from the exaggeration of the difference between the Oriental and Occidental types of mind. The Oriental mind is described as so peculiar in its methods of thought, so moulded by the ideals of religion which have obtained sway over it through long generations, that it is hopeless to think of instilling into it what are called purely Western ideas of religious thought and life. And no doubt the Oriental mind is strangely different from the European. No doubt also in virtue of its habits the Indian or the Chinaman may find it exceedingly difficult to assimilate the theology of the historical Christian church. But this does not prove that Christianity is so unsuited to the Oriental

mind that the latter will not be persuaded to
receive it.

For, in the first place, we must remember that
Christianity had its origin in the East, and that
the Christian Scriptures are full of modes of thought
and mystic conceptions which claim close kinship
with those of the Oriental religions.

And, in the second place, a double inquiry
suggests itself regarding this Oriental type of
mind. To begin with, one must inquire whether
its modes of working are superior to those which
the European mind has attained. It is not at
all obvious that, so far as the Oriental mind is
incapable of appreciating the severe scientific
methods of the European, it is not inferior to
the latter. Its characteristic elements may,
perhaps, be described as, first, thinking through
imagery. No doubt the mind that is content to do
its thinking by similes and metaphors does obtain
frequent illuminations. The contemplation and
comparison of conceptions which in themselves
seem diverse may gradually bring to light
apparent points of similarity and suggest thoughts
both novel and beautiful. But this kind of thinking, which pervades the sacred books of the East
from end to end, and may be said to be characteristic
of the Oriental type of mind, has very decided
limitations. There is no certainty regarding the
conclusions to which it leads. There is required
the more sober work of analysis, the use of some
standards of reality, the appeal to some facts whose
nature is already independently ascertained, ere

this kind of thinking can be considered of objective value. As a matter of fact, it has resulted in making Oriental religion so intensely individualistic as it has become even in its Buddhistic form. Then, further, there is that element of the Oriental type of mind, known as the mystical. To be sure, Europe has had its mystics, and some of them are not unworthy to be compared with the most sublime of Indian thinkers and teachers. But in the East, mysticism, the sense of inward personal contact with the ideal, the infinite,—the submission of the mind and heart to the sway of thoughts which are vast, indefinite, which seem to bring the individual soul into contact, vague but real, inexpressible but sweet and entrancing, with the All-soul, the One, the Eternal,—this has been at once the strength and the weakness of Oriental thought. It is open to the severest criticism, not only on intellectual grounds, but for its religious and moral effects, for its easy exaggeration of a truth into a most dangerous if impalpable superstition. Then, again, this Oriental thought is distinguished by its lack of dependence upon the historical and actual. Its religions profess to be grounded upon events in the past, but so little has the Oriental mind cared for this, so little are the facts essential to the religion, that they have become overlaid with all manner of legend and folly. The individual founder of the religion is not necessary to its continuance; he passes away, and henceforth becomes the subject of popular, endless, and entirely uncritical description and faith.

Over against these elements of the Oriental mind we place those of the Western mind, with its clinging to the concrete, which is at once the fountain and the result of its marvellous attainments, and its careful scrutiny of history. One young Japanese scholar, after a prolonged course of study in America, returned to his native land to become a professor. He resolved to apply the scientific methods of inquiry which he had learned abroad to the history of his ancestral religions. The results were so surprising, and produced such dismay among his pupils and in the minds of the authorities, that he had to cease from that kind of work. It may be said, of course, that similar methods of coercion have been applied by ecclesiastical authorities to those who investigated the history of Christian origins and Christian documents, and who reported in terms not favourable to traditional ideas of these matters. But it has to be remembered, on the other hand, that while in Japan the investigation was killing, and is killing, the faith of educated people in those stories, the far deeper investigations into Christian history have not ended in that way. In fact, so valuable have historical studies proved to the life of the church, that to-day they are pursued with a thoroughness and on a scale unsurpassed by anything in the intellectual life of man.

The enormous importance which the Christian religion has come to attach to exactness of historical statement, arises from the fact that this religion is nothing without its history. The powers that

to-day work in the human heart are said by it to
be vitally connected with events and deeds which
occurred amongst men. Without the appropriation
of the latter a man remains dead to the former.

These features which indicate the immense
superiority of the European over the Asiatic mind
raise now the second inquiry, whether that
which is likely to take place, instead of being the
absorption of Christianity into the vague cavern
of the "Oriental type of mind," will not be, to
change the metaphor, the emancipation of that
mind from its age-long fetters. The experience of
the Education Department of the Government of
India, as well as that of the missionary church,
seems to indicate that European science and
philosophy, as well as religion, are about to produce
in the Eastern world one of the swiftest and
mightiest intellectual revolutions known to history.
That contributions of value will be made from the
East to the stock of the world's wisdom, and to
man's spiritual insight, goes without saying. The
church is ready to welcome them all. But it is
practically certain that the church of Christ and
the European mind will, as regards modes of
thought and forms of religious life, give infinitely
more than they will ever receive. Signs of this
are abundant enough already. For, after all,
something like two millions of Asiatics have become
converts to Christianity, and there are many
thousands of Indian men whose minds are
saturated with the methods and spirit of Occidental
science and philosophy. That the result is at

present confusing, and is accompanied by some phenomena which are ludicrous, as well as startling, in the crude theories and expressions of opinion characteristic of the young Indian who has slightly tasted European modes of thought, is only what we ought to expect.   But the work of transformation is proceeding.   It may not be too bold to assert that, as a result, the leading races of the world will receive one more proof that their progress in philosophy, in science, and in religion has been real, by finding that their communication of the wealth so hardly won is making the poorer people of the Orient rich after the same fashion.

CHAPTER IX

THE MISSIONARY AS SAVIOUR

In the preceding pages we have discussed missionary activity in various phases, and the influence of the missionary movement upon the heathen world in various directions. We have seen the preacher of Christ as the pioneer, opening up new countries and bringing them into living connection with the centres of civilisation. We have seen him as the linguist, translator, and author; we have watched him as the educator, the overseer, the adviser of native teachers, converts, and chieftains. Such a survey might suggest to some minds that the aim of the missionary is to be found in these activities and labours, and that the final reason for this great movement must be discovered in its social and visible effects. It would be, however, a great mistake to suppose that the missionary engages in any of these forms of service to mankind for its own sake. He knows their value and rejoices in it; he would be the last to depreciate any portion of the work which he has done, or the results which he has seen in the midst of a heathen civilisation. But these activities have all been entered upon as means towards another end, which is the supreme object of his ambition. They may all be described as the means or the adjuncts or the consequences of his devotion to that one aim.

The missionaries have gone out to do the work of saviours. They believe that this is the one purpose for which it is worth their while to sacrifice their whole careers, and, if necessary, yield up their lives. Their whole object, the one constant endeavour which is ever present to their minds, is the making of individual heathen men and women into Christian converts. For this they translate and educate, for this they travel and suffer, organise and preach. They desire to bring men to that act which the Christian world calls faith in Christ, to that accompanying experience which the Christian world calls the new birth. In the pursuit of this aim, they believe that they are acting in the spirit and following the example of Jesus Christ, their Master. He spoke of men as lost, as separate from God, like the prodigal from his father; and the supreme aim of His ministry and death was to bring this condition to an end, to save the lost, to arouse the trust and love of man towards God. This aim passed from Him to His apostles; they too went everywhere seeking to persuade men to believe in Christ, to enter upon those relations with God which He had made possible. The missionary, as a man who himself has received this consciousness of the new life, and finds himself in relations of trust and harmony towards God, strives to do for the heathen world the same work which

the apostles accomplished for so many in the
Græco-Roman world, in the name of Christ.   To
the mind of the missionary, the word "lost," which
fell from the lips of Jesus, describes accurately, if
dismally, the condition of heathen men and women.
Having received something of the Spirit of Christ
into his heart, he yearns to be the means of deliver-
ing some men and women out of their dread
condition into the life of divine fellowship.   It is
this alone which seems so glorious a work, that for
its sake he will give up all that he counts dear,
as we have seen, and toil in all directions at any
task which promises to aid him in this supreme
purpose.

If we examine the journals, letters, and speeches
of evangelical missionaries of any section of the
Christian church, working amongst the children
of any race, we find that it is for this they watch
and work through all the years.   When Henry
Martyn, after landing in India, expressed the desire
to "burn out for God," his thought was fixed upon
this work of a saviour; when Carey spent his
forty years and more in toil of many kinds, his
eyes were ever directed forward towards the
persuasion of the Indian peoples to become believers
in Jesus Christ; when J. G. Paton remained on
Tanna after the death of his wife, lonely, crushed
and fever-stricken, when he turned a deaf ear to
proposals that he should leave the island for a
time, when he saw the ship sail out to sea, and
went from the shore to his desolate house again,
that which was in his mind, which shone like a

beacon of hope before the eyes of his soul, was the prospect of watching some fierce and brutal islander begin to see the light, to feel the stings of conscience, to seek the forgiveness of God, and find the transforming fellowship of Jesus Christ; when a man so full of domestic tenderness and sympathetic love as James Gilmour, gave himself up to the miserable loneliness of those long winters in Mongolia, when he stood under his little awning on the public street day after day, selling medicines and books, and speaking with all who would approach him, what did he hunger most for, but the sight of some dull, self-satisfied Mongol heart, broken down by the power of the gospel of Jesus Christ ?

As the missionary directs all his energies towards this one end, he finds that there are two agencies of a personal nature through which he may hope to succeed.   In the first place, he appears amongst these strange races simply as a witness to the experiences which the Christian religion has brought to himself.   Formal preaching is of no avail, regular instruction has no place, until some have been persuaded and have entered into sympathy with his thought.   In order to create that sympathy, he must be able to describe and bear personal testimony to certain great moral and spiritual experiences, whose value will be evident or can be made evident to his heathen auditors. " My experience of Christ " is the text of all his preaching.   I have heard one of the most successful missionaries in India say, that when he enters a new village and gathers a few people round him, he begins by telling them what Jesus Christ has done for him personally. It is his peace and hope and love felt toward God, his assurance of the Fatherhood of God, to which he directs attention. Then he asks them if their religion has done that for them. But, in the second place, his teaching must receive illumination from his own character and life. For, as it has been well put, "the Moslem must first find Christ in the missionary, before he can find Him in Jesus of Nazareth."[1] Here in a Christian land we are perhaps able to distinguish between the value of a minister's teaching and that of his personal character; we have learned from repeated and bitter experience, not to make the truth of the teaching and its influence upon our hearts to depend exclusively upon its fulfilment by the preacher himself. And yet who has not felt that added force which is given to the exhortation of the plainest man, when we realise that his own character and life accord with the ideal which he is urging upon us? In a heathen land they are unable to make any such distinctions; the missionary must himself be an evidence of Christianity. He must reveal the gospel at work; in his own relations with the natives, he must exemplify the relations in which he says that Jesus Christ stands towards all men. The mind which was in Christ must be also obviously in him. The result may be that the heathen come first of all to trust him as their friend, ere they can be

[1] President Washburn in *Missions at Home and Abroad*, p. 154.

convinced that his friendliness is derived from another. But by whatever steps the native mind may move towards the great conclusion, it is practically impossible that a man, calling himself a missionary of Christ, who is notoriously unlike Him, should lead them through those steps. It may be that the conclusion reached is after all not that which the missionary desires. A man may be content to say, as an accomplished Indian Mohammedan is reported to have said,—"I think Jesus Christ must have been a wonderful man. He must have been something like Mr. Hewlett of Benares,"—naming a well-known missionary. But whether the great desire of the missionary is attained or not, this one thing he knows is essential to its attainment, that, amidst the many disappointments which he meets, and the many trials of his patience, he should manifest the strong self-control and sympathetic meekness of his Master. His aim, as it has been well expressed, must have nothing sectarian in it. This, too, is part of the character which he must display, viz., the charity that overpasses differences of opinion with his fellow-Christians. The unity of spirit which, as a matter of fact, *is* being exercised in so inspiring a fashion by the missionaries of the various evangelical denominations, as they work together in foreign lands, is essential to the task of winning the heathen to faith. "The true aim of missionary work is to make Christ known to the world. Nothing is foreign to this work which reveals His spirit or the characteristics of His kingdom, and nothing is essential to it which is peculiar to a sect, a class, or a civilisation." [1]

These facts receive their best illustration, many think, in the work and influence of the medical missionary. This department of missionary enterprise has developed with extraordinary rapidity during the latter half of this century; and it has proved to be one of the most effective weapons which can be employed in the heathen world. Whereas fifty years ago they were exceedingly few and far between, there are now throughout the world over four hundred fully qualified medical missionaries, ninety of whom are women. They, with a large number of assistants, are said to treat more than a million persons every year. In India alone there are eighty-seven male and fifty-seven female missionaries, who have trained and employ one hundred and sixty-eight native medical assistants, and who carry on their labours in connection with forty-eight hospitals and eighty-seven dispensaries. It is unnecessary to enter with any detail upon the significance of the work which the medical missionary does. He himself sees in his ministry the nearest possible human approach to that of Jesus. This healer of the sick means not only to relieve suffering, but in doing so to reveal the grace of God, to touch some responsive chord in darkened hearts, and win from them appreciation of the divine love. In the daily work carried on amongst innumerable outdoor patients, the oppor-

[1] President Washburn of Constantinople, in *Missions at Home and Abroad*, p. 164.

tunity may not be good for that awakening of personal and intelligent interest in Christian experience; but these transient patients, by going forth to sound abroad the praises of the missionary's skill and the missionary's friendliness, do valuable work in stimulating the interest of the community far and wide. It is, however, amongst those who become inmates of a hospital, or whom the Christian doctor is able to treat for prolonged periods in their homes, that the greatest results are obtained. That mutual understanding and sympathy which springs up always between physician and patient is a new experience to the native. The fact that the medical missionary accepts no personal reward for his exhausting and inexplicable self-denial is a new cause of wonder. The fact that most of these cases are serious, that the sufferer is on the borderland between life and death, and that the whole problem of existence and personal responsibility is congenial to his state of mind, give the alert and eager herald of Christ opportunity for bearing witness to the name of his Master in its significance for his own heart and for the destiny of all men. The results which flow from this kind of work are in many cases most startling. Stories are innumerable, from all parts of the world, of the effects produced, in places far from the scene of the medical mission, by the example and teaching of converts who have gone to their distant homes from its hospital. From such small beginnings large churches have grown, new mission fields have been opened up, over and over again.

By none has the work of the medical missionary been more beautifully portrayed than by Dr. Post of Beirut, himself one of the most successful physician-evangelists. "There is a language," he says, "which all can understand, and which carries a message which every man cares sooner or later to hear. From the moment the medical missionary sets foot on his chosen field he is master of this universal language, this unspoken tongue of the heart, and welcome to the homes of strangers. The simple Arab lifts for him the curtain of his goat's hair tent and bids him enter. The mandarin calls him to his palace, the peasant begs him to come to his lowly cabin, the Brahmin leads him to the recesses of his zenana. He stands before kings, and governors escort him with squadrons of cavalry, or take him to and fro in their gunboats or their barges of state. Kings build hospitals for him, and the rulers of the earth aid him with their treasures and their power. . . . You take the Bible to the heathen, and he may spit upon it or burn it, or throw it aside as worthless or harmful. You preach the gospel to him, and he may regard you as a hireling who makes preaching a trade. He may meet your arguments with sophistry, your appeals with a sneer. You educate him, and he may change from a heathen to an infidel. But heal his bodily ailment in the name of Christ, and you are sure at least that he will love you and bless you, and that all you say will have to him a meaning and a power not conveyed by other lips." [1]

[1] In *Missions at Home and Abroad,* pp. 346, 347.

The medical missionary seldom or never allows himself to forget that his life has been given to what has aptly been called "the double cure." [1] He is appointed to heal the bodies of men in his hospital as a missionary of Christ, in order that through the avenues of sympathy and trust thus opened, he may be able to secure for his patients the healing of the deeper and more dismal diseases of the soul. He is unfaithful to his calling if the latter is neglected under the stress of the former labour. Where the two aspects of his work are kept well in view, and arrangements are made for the wise and affectionate instruction of the inmates of the hospital, the number of converts to the Christian faith is often very great.

One of the most striking results of the medical missionary movement has been, that, through the work of these Christian men and women, admission has been obtained to the homes of the noble and the wealthy in Oriental lands. The homes of the Chinese dignitaries, the zenana of the Brahmin, open their doors — uneasily it may be, and reluctantly at first—to the medical missionary. To all others they are sternly closed, and their inmates remain beyond the reach of Christian teachers; but when the stern demands of disease or the approaching horror of the shadow of death have compelled the patient and the anxious relatives alike to break away from tradition and invite the help of the foreign doctor, then these secluded hearts are brought within the sound of that most potent moral

[1] *John Kenneth Mackenzie*, App. IV., pp. 400 ff.

and spiritual influence in the history of man, the story of Jesus Christ.

When the missionary, by means of his personal testimony and teaching, and the influence of his own character and life, has won some converts to the faith of Jesus Christ, they begin to live the life of fellowship, of closer intercourse with one another in the brotherhood of an organised church. When the life of such a young community begins to manifest its own features in a heathen land, one fact becomes apparent which seems to be of great significance, as it seems to be of a unique character. It is this, that the religious experience of the converts from heathendom to-day is, in all essentials, identical with that described in the New Testament as possessed by the earliest followers of the apostolic faith. We are accustomed to hear much said concerning the enormous developments which have taken place in church life. Emphasis is laid upon the difference between a cathedral service in London and the service in a little room or a synagogue which Paul may have conducted; or men contrast him, the homeless herald of Jesus Christ, who gave up wealth and position, with a well-paid minister or a high dignitary of modern evangelical Christendom. Or, again, a contrast is drawn between the stately and dignified intellectualism or the refined and subtle spiritual teaching of a modern sermon, and that sympathetic, direct, passionate, and brief outburst which seems to have been the main form of exhortation amongst the primitive Christians. Some profess to find part of the secret of what they consider to be a deep divergence from primitive Christianity by describing the Sermon on the Mount as expressing the true spirit of the latter, while the elaborate creeds of the church are said to be the fetters which have interfered with the church's freedom and impaired its influence over man. These contrasts, whether they be exaggerated and misleading or not, after all do not deal with the substance of Christian experience. The modern missionary movement has served more than any other event to make this manifest. A visit to these fields will reveal phenomena exactly, sometimes ludicrously, similar to certain of those depicted in the New Testament, as belonging to the cruder stages of church life. But the observer and student of Christian experience cannot escape the similarity which there is between the deeper, the real essence of the new life, as that appears to-day, and as it appeared eighteen hundred years ago. Then, as to-day, men entered into the consciousness of new life through the narrow gate of misery about their sin, and repentance; then, as now, men became persuaded that Jesus Christ is the appointed Saviour of the world, through whom deliverance could be obtained; then, as now, they saw in His cross the supreme ground and proof of the mercy of God and the distress of man; then, as now, they passed through the time of struggle with self to the time of trust; then, as now, they received what we call the Holy Spirit; a new feeling regarding God swept over them; a new consciousness concerning

14

their whole condition as moral and responsible beings was awakened within them ; a new sense of the worth of man filled their hearts ; a kindlier love for him who is their brother in this experience, and a yearning pity for the men who have tasted it not, were borne in upon them. Then, as now, these fundamental forms of Christian experience, in varying proportions but in essential identity, gave proof to the Christian converts themselves that God had taken possession of their hearts, and roused in the outside world a feeling either of awe, or contempt mingled with wonder, at this thing that was happening amongst men.

To put the matter shortly, it may be said that the same ethical and religious phenomena are being produced by the preaching of Jesus Christ as the Saviour of men in the nineteenth century as in the first century. The most solemn, and, apart from the gospel, the most crushing and dismaying facts are turned into grounds of joy, and awaken thoughts of triumph. The judgment of the holy and righteous God, the sense of sin, the approach of death, are transmuted in their significance for the Christian heart. The dawn of faith, the quickening of conscience, the inflow of joy, the outflow of love, the experience of a moral energy,—these are the permanent characteristics of the Christian religion. All these are effects which everywhere follow upon the preaching of the name of Jesus Christ. That this preaching is conducted in various languages, or that there are differences of standpoint on many matters more or less important amongst the preachers of the gospel, does not destroy the identity of the message which they have presented through all the centuries and throughout the world. The words of Jesus and His apostles come home to them all with an authority before which they bow. They universally find in Holy Writ the fittest expressions of their own thoughts, and the clearest descriptions of their own experience, in relation to God and eternal life.

These facts seem to demand a most thorough investigation even from those who deny that the Christian faith is grounded in truth, and should receive an explanation more adequate than any which has yet been offered to us. The mere denial that the Christian faith is true is not sufficient; the scientific task remains. And that task consists in explaining how these religious phenomena have persisted during two thousand years, how it is that they have had such influence over the development of all sides of European civilisation, and how it is that to-day, throughout the world, races of the most divergent intellectual and religious types are being brought into a fundamental unity of religious life by the same means. This is the effect of the work of missionaries, as the saviours of men. Their intense passion for what they call "saving the lost" lies behind this movement, and the movement is successful in their eyes only in so far as they behold individual men and women brought into this religious relation to Jesus Christ, and through Him to the living God.

It is this religious element which, both as the cause of the missionary's devotion and the centre of the native convert's new experience and new insight, is the spring of all those events and changes, so innumerable, so varied, so vitally important for the history of mankind, which we call the missionary movement. No theory can possibly explain either the rise of that movement or its remarkable results which does not give full weight to the religious consciousness of the missionary, — for this alone gives him at once his motive and his aim,—and to the religious consciousness of the convert, which constitutes the missionary's triumph and is the seed of progress.

In the missionary fields of the evangelical churches, it is the universal custom to baptise and to receive formally as communicants only those who have become the subjects of this religious experience. Not because they have been taught in the schools or have been healed by medical missionaries, not because they have adopted European clothing or enlarged their houses, or have tried to use any other of the personal and domestic adjuncts of civilised life, are they added to the church. To-day, as in the earliest weeks of the church's life, those that are being added are those that give evidence that they are "being saved." As this is the aim of the missionary's labour, it is the starting-point of the church's life in these lands. When a few converts have been gathered and organised, then the spread of Christianity in that region assumes more or less distinctly the form which it has attained in older lands, viz., that of self-propagation through local communities. The members of the church are banded together for aggressive purposes. Whether the community ignores them or not, they never ignore the community. They stand together and labour individually and collectively for the further-ance of the gospel. The history of the church is continuous from the days of the apostles to the formation of the latest little group of disciples in Central Africa or Central China. From community to community the light has spread, and from each community it shines out upon the surrounding world. The ambition of the missionary churches of Christendom is to see the church of Christ so established and developed in India and China and Africa, and in all other parts of the earth, that at last the word "foreign missionary" shall cease to have a meaning. The church will have become as truly indigenous in all those lands as it now seems to be in Germany or England or in the United States of America. No earthly force or organisa-tion is at work seeking this end; no temporal ambi-tion or scheme, whether of ecclesiastical politicians or statesmanlike dignitaries, will account for the self-propagation of the Christian church. It is a spontaneous, perpetual, irrepressible outflow of its deepest life. What is the law of the spread of this communion of believers, as they love to call it, throughout the world? Surely, in the extra-ordinary phenomena which are before our eyes in the mission fields of the world, evidence can be discovered which suggests or compels the right and inevitable conclusion. The old formulæ of Gibbon, in his description of the spread of the early church, although true in part, are inadequate for the statement of this law. No mere assumption that these phenomena belong to the realm of superstition, and that, therefore, the sober-minded and advanced thinker may afford to despise them, can possibly be treated with respect to-day. The spread of the church in our day has been characterised by many of the same features which are familiar to the student of the first Christian centuries. The same power which gave it the victory over the heathen world of those times must be the secret of its triumphant progress to-day.

Many depreciate its victories by pointing to the unworthy life of some of its converts and adherents in Christian and heathen lands. This unworthiness is undeniable and deplorable, but it only makes the victory the more remarkable. Professor Sohm, in his vivid little book, the *Outlines of Church History*, has described the matter with so much eloquence and authority that I cannot refrain from quoting the following passage in full : —"And yet the Church has remained unconquerable. The marvel of Christianity and its grandest achievement is just this : that it could not be destroyed, that it won the victory although so miserably represented by its followers. Apostasy, weakness, and sin have had no power to destroy the imperishable strength of Christianity. It became secularised, yet it still remained a leaven to leaven the whole world. It was betrayed by a large[1] number of its followers, yet there abode within it that spirit which, in one little band of the chosen, in spite of sin and error, was powerful enough to overcome the world, and, through its glorious example of martyrdom, to arouse the spirit of resistance even in the ranks of the luke-warm, the wavering, and the faint. By this time Christianity was no more than an unknown religion against which the falsest and most hideous scandals were circulated and believed (as in the first and second centuries). The spirit of Christianity had become *visible*, and it stretched forth its shelter-ing wing over its followers. . . . Already, not only were the convictions of the best minds of the age opposed to the State, but it had against it the whole of the spiritual power wherewith Christianity (once seen as it truly is) influences even the outer world. The spiritual power was made manifest, and developed all its forces to the utmost, in spite of the weakness of its followers. Through all the shades and darkness which surround us in the history of the Christian church, there breaks forth evermore victorious—like the sun going forth in his strength, rending the clouds asunder and gleaming through the rift, now in one place, now in another — the im-perishable light of true Christianity. So it was

[1] The translation which I use here says, "by the *greater* number." Professor Sohm in 6th, 7th, and 8th Edd. says, "Von einer grossen Zahl."

then. The church conquered, not because of the Christians, but in spite of them — through the power of the gospel."[1] Now the gospel is the announcement that men may have individual and collective fellowship with God through faith in Jesus Christ. The experience which that announcement is spreading among men is the one great aim for which the missionary labours as a saviour of men, and from that experience all the great branches of the tree of human progress draw their life, their nourishment, and their fruitage.

[1] Rudolph Sohm, in *Outlines of Church History*, pp. 21, 22.

CHAPTER X

It is not at all a simple task to describe what is meant by "The Progress of Man." The idea floats hazily before our eyes, and we all speak of it very confidently as well as very constantly ; but we do not find it easy to name its elements and conditions. It seems natural to speak of it when we are discussing certain aspects of social change or national expansion, and specific forms of progress can be easily selected and named. For example, it is no doubt a form of progress that we should be able to travel at sixty instead of six miles an hour. It is also progress in the eyes of many that our legislators in city and nation should be chosen directly by the people. It is also progress that each morning our newspaper should lie on the breakfast table, putting the news of the world's chief events during the previous twenty-four hours before us. To name the printing-press and electricity and steamships and representative government and popular education, is to name the signs and the proofs of some kind of progress. But when we have named them all separately, can we put them all together into one concept, and say exactly wherein the progress of man consists? A recent writer repeats with emphasis and frequency that "evolution is universal, but progress very rare."[1] It becomes us, therefore, to ask by what signs we are to recognise progress, and to distinguish that form of evolution which promises an endless, or at least a real, advance from those forms which have passed or are destined to pass away, as mere oscillations in human history.

There are three conditions, two of which must be fulfilled ere there can be progress in any section of the race, and the third of which must be added ere we can speak of the progress of man as a whole.

It must be evident, to begin with, that evolution implies, as Mr. Spencer has so fully argued in his essay on *Universal Progress*, the elaboration of social relations. There are those who feel impatient at the intricate and almost bewildering multiplication of functions which has been going on in the body politic during the very rapid changes of this century. But as a matter of fact this division results from the vast increase of work which is now needed to meet the demands of accumulating population and to disseminate the benefits of

[1] *Introduction to the History of Religion*, by J. B. Jevons, p. 5. Compare with Mr. Jevons's form of statement, the late Walter Bagehot's words in his essay on "Verifiable Progress": "A stationary state is by far the most frequent condition of man, as far as history describes that condition; the progressive state is only a rare and an occasional exception."—*Works* (American ed.), vol. iv., p. 583.

mechanical inventions. At the same time, it is a question whether this growing complexity itself, the mere subdivison of functions in society, is the exact essence of man's progress. Mr. Spencer's essay does not seem to meet that problem. He simply assumes that the increasing "coherent heterogeneity" of the organs of life, which is the mark of organic evolution, is the fundamental characteristic of social progress. Mr. Spencer's words are : "It is settled beyond all dispute that organic progress consists in a change from the homogeneous to the heterogeneous." "The law of organic progress is the law of all progress." "The evolution of the simple into the complex, through successive differentiations, holds throughout."[1] We need not despair of some day seeing this advance in the complexity of social life traced to man's moral nature and even to his religious instincts; so, its place in the idea of progress will be more clearly defined than has been done or attempted by Mr. Spencer.

If we conceive of a tribe of people as living, unwarlike, and in the enjoyment of a comparatively simple organisation, a change in the condition of its life can only occur in one of two ways. Either the advent of strangers with a higher form of civilisation will at once begin to break up and alter its organisation, or the rise of fresh ambitions from within will have the same effect. The organisation of many an African or Polynesian tribe is being affected in the former way to-day. The organisation of English social life was affected

[1] *Universal Progress*, by Herbert Spencer, pp. 3 ff.

in the latter way by the awakening which followed
the introduction of steam engines. In the former
case the tribe usually becomes demoralised, and
what is called "decadent," unless there come, along
with the new social demands, higher personal
character to meet them. The ordinary unchristianised, that is, unmoralised, native cannot as a matter
of fact sustain the stress put upon him by the more
elaborate social system which is growing around
him. We are apt to blame the native thus placed
for lack of intelligence, whereas what is wrong is
the lack of that sense of responsibility, that moral
courage, that self-respect which would enable him
to take a definite place and fulfil a real function,
however humble, in the life of the reorganised
social system. It is the absence of moral qualities
which keeps the Zulu unprogressive; nay, which
makes him seem to be more of an animal than
before, when a civilised government has taken
charge of his tribe and himself.

But the connection between growth in social
organisation — coherent heterogeneity of social
functions—and moral character may be seen still
more clearly by watching the experience of large
cities in America, where great masses of immigrant
people, with innumerable forms of social, family
and religious traditions, are thrown together and
compelled to organise themselves into a civilised
community. The evidence proves beyond all
possibility of refutation that, when the city is
governed by unprincipled men, mostly saloon-
keepers, the government assumes an oligarchic

form. The so-called political parties fall into the hands of a few men, who practically re-elect themselves or kindred spirits year after year. The democratic form of government is then really in a state of suspended animation, having a name to live, say, on the Fourth of July. The result is this, that the differentiation of civic functions is arrested or hindered in its growth. Men are appointed to offices who are not fitted for them, and who are liable to dismissal at the next election. Hence there is inefficient work done. The organisation does not grow, functions are not differentiated, to meet the ever-growing life of the social organism. Streets are allowed to remain in disrepair which ought to be repaved, refuse accumulates to the danger of health, crime increases so that burglary insurance companies may refuse to do business in such a city, bribery and corruption lay their hands so heavily on business that some men try to move their concerns out of it. If this process were allowed to go on indefinitely, no city could fail to be utterly ruined. Happily these American cities have a very great amount of civic enthusiasm which, while generally torpid, is aroused at times to speak and act so that the worst events are prevented, and progress of a retarded degree is maintained pretty steadily.

What I have meant to say is this, that the increase of organisation, which for Mr. Spencer seems to *constitute* progress, cannot be the ultimate fact, since it appears to be absolutely dependent upon growth of character. And the experience of, say, New York and Chicago, proves that, *first*, failure in the character of its rulers tends evidently to dislocate the organisation of the city, and so hinders that differentiation of functions which, I prefer to say, *marks* progress; while, *secondly*, the demand for better organisation—which to a large extent and necessarily takes the form of the civil service movement, because that best secures differentiation of functions—always begins by securing morally decent legislators, and always springs from citizens of high character and religious faith.

There is another aspect of man's evolution which we must look at, namely, the great and wonderful power which has been gained over nature. The effects of man's continuous triumph over the forces of the physical world are most varied. The most obvious results are the increase of the wealth of the average citizen in Europe and America, and the spread of luxury through the community. Only the least thoughtful will be likely to insist that these things form the essence of progress. And yet it would be almost equally thoughtless to say that they have nothing to do with it. When one thinks of the marvellous scientific attainments of the last few centuries, the daring which conceived and the thrilling genius which has accomplished the binding of all lands together by ocean cables and steamships and railroads, which speak now of regulating the fall of heaven's rain and of sailing through the air as safely and more swiftly than upon the waters—when we think of these things, we can hardly resist the conclusion that man's triumph over nature constitutes another, the second, essential element in that which we call his progress. The facts become almost startling when we realise that, through his power over her forces, nature has become in a new and most real manner an extension of man's self. In earliest days his self was absorbed in nature, lost he seemed to be amid the whirl of irresistible and inscrutable forces. Then the consciousness of war awoke, when man's soul seemed to be striving against a world peopled with evil powers; that was the age of crushing superstitions, of witchcraft and incantations. Then gradually nature began to be understood and conquered. The forces that hitherto only appalled began to be used, and once more nature seems to be a part of man's self, her forces the instruments of his purpose. Has this progress in science and the practical arts any living connection with morality and religion?

I believe it can be proved that science owes her deepest and most influential conceptions, those which have most profoundly given her life and health, to religion, nay, even to theology. Science is the daughter not only of faith but of theological discussion. It is the habit of some more talkative and self-conscious wooers of that popular maiden to deny her descent or deride her mother. But the mother is very patient, and, for all her occasional scoldings, loves her offspring. The wiser students of nature, and they in sufficient numbers through every generation, own the deep connection that exists between progress in science and faith in the illuminating ideals, the glorious realities of the spiritual world.

The question can be dealt with in a more concrete way. The triumphs of science are of two kinds, theoretical and practical, and progress in both kinds is very closely allied with character, with the moral condition of society. It is well known that the men who have done most as investigators of nature have almost invariably borne high personal characters. They have been clean and straightforward, courageous men. The fact is, that no other kind of man can go far in the pursuit of any science. When his departures from rectitude become serious and habitual, they wreck his work, almost as soon as they wreck that of a minister of religion. But, further, it is obvious that when science becomes practical, her triumphs become immediately connected with the moral condition of the community. At once, for example, there is a demand for increased numbers of specialists in various forms of skilled labour,—the differentiation of social functions. Every fresh invention demands and effects a reorganisation of society, more or less extensive, according to its importance. But the multiplication of departments, as we have already seen, depends upon the moral character of the community and of the rulers whom it elects. For example, the holders of a monopoly in a city can by means of bribery prevent the adoption of some improved means of transit or illumination which would interfere with their profits. We know that where a sweating system prevails, invention is retarded; honest payment for honest work stimulates invention. And similarly we know that if a community becomes very careful about protecting the rights of the working men and women and children, the extra demands thus made upon employers tend always to improve machinery, and so to cheapen manufactures, and so to increase the material welfare of the community.

We are thus brought face to face with the fact, not that material wealth is progress, but that progress in the widest and fullest sense must include that mastery of the forces of nature which produces material wealth. It seems also clear that this advance in science is closely dependent upon progress in the moral character of the community.

The third condition of universal human progress remains to be named. The progress which we hope for and whose nature we are trying to understand is the progress of man, of the race as such. We are not concerned with this or that nation, whether ancient or modern, and its supremacy over others in this or that direction. Many great nations have fallen into decay, many types of civilisation have been more or less completely obliterated, because they lacked something which would have enabled them to absorb and elevate the savage hordes who overwhelmed them. Some types have reached a certain height and then ceased to make progress, evidently because they, too, lacked something which would have carried them farther on. A new vision and a new hope

15

have been slowly dawning on our inapprehensive minds. The vision is that of all nations drawn irresistibly into one common life; the hope is that the forces which make the nations one will prove adequate to secure a permanent progress. The nineteenth century opened when that vision was before few, if any, minds, whether of poet or saint. Men could not think of the one life of mankind, with Africa an unknown darkness, India in pristine disorder, China enjoying still her ancient slumber and her impenetrable dreams, Polynesia but a number of scattered spots of human degradation in the Pacific Ocean. To-day we are gazing on the rapid realisation of the unity of mankind in commerce, politics, education, and religion. These forces are daily increasing the communion of all parts of the world with one another, and deepening the interdependence of all races and nations.

Now this feature of history is of the utmost importance for our right understanding of the progress of man. Without this fellowship of all peoples the progress made by any portion of mankind must be incomplete and its permanence uncertain. All must at last go forward together, if any may claim that they are moving toward the ideal. The brotherhood of man as an actual fact is essential to the real and endless advance of humanity.

So far we have seen that the growth of social organisation, of power over nature, and of the unity of all nations, are essential to a true conception of the progress of man. We have also seen that these forms of advance are all closely dependent upon what we have called character.   What does that mean ?

Writers who occupy such divergent standpoints as T. H. Green and M. Elisée Reclus agree in laying much emphasis upon character as necessary to a true theory of progress.   Says the former: " The spiritual progress of mankind is thus an unmeaning phrase, unless it means a progress *of* personal character and *to* personal character—a progress of which feeling, thinking, and willing subjects are the agents and sustainers, and of which each step is a fuller realisation of the capacities of such subjects.   It is simply unintelligible unless understood to be in the direction of more perfect forms of personal life."   Green makes another remark which shows that he does not think of "spiritual progress " as simply one among other aspects or forms of progress.   " If it were not for certain demands of the spirit which is ourselves, the notion of human progress could never occur to us." [1]   M. Reclus puts the matter in the following way in a recent article :—Progress " ought above all to be understood as a complete development of the individual, comprehending the improvement of the physical being in strength, beauty, grace, longevity, material enrichment, and increase of knowledge—in fine, the perfecting of character, the becoming more noble, more generous, and more devoted.   So considered, the progress of the individual is identified with that of society,

[1] T. H. Green's *Prolegomena to Ethics*, p. 195.

united more and more intimately in a powerful solidarity." [1]

And yet again, Professor Huxley says with equal emphasis that "social progress means a checking of the cosmic process at every step and the substitution for it of another, which may be called the ethical process." [2] These thinkers, working from very different philosophical and religious standpoints, arrive unanimously at the conviction that the moral life of man is the region where we may find at once the source, the essence, and the test of progress. We have been in part helped to understand, or at anyrate to see this, in preceding paragraphs. We have found not only that the three main elements and collateral results of progress, viz., the elaboration of social relations, the triumph over nature, and the unification of the race are naturally connected and very largely interdependent, but that, each and all, they are in some vital manner dependent upon "character." If now we would push our inquiry further, and ask what we mean by "character," why progress in *that* should be progress itself and should secure a correlative progress in other directions, we find ourselves face to face with another of the most elusive and yet fascinating of problems. We can only deal with a small section of it here.

Manifestly, when we speak of "character," or of "the ethical process," we are thinking of *good*

[1] Article on "Progress" in *Contemporary Review*, December 1896, p. 762.

[2] Huxley's *Evolution and Ethics*, p. 81.

character, or of a process through which higher personal relations are being arrived at and realised by any community. The members of a group of people, whether a little tribe or a great nation, are possessed of the conviction that certain habits of life, towards which it is easy to drift, are disgraceful and dangerous, and that certain other kinds of conduct or personal relationship are pure and noble. If the average man in the community is unable to speak definitely of these moral ideals as ideals, not having had the training or the meditative capacity to think of them, he is conscious of their attraction or repulsion as a kind of feeling or social instinct. There are, however, men and women to be found in almost every community whose work it is to propagate throughout the social system an enthusiasm for these ideals and a sense of their high and indisputable authority.

It will be found, of course, that the ideals which any group of people cherish, are very closely connected with their material welfare or even with their very existence as a community. In early Rome, for example, the conditions of life were such that the city could only live by maintaining certain strict and noble laws of family and civic life. The emphasis which they laid upon filial reverence, making it almost the equivalent of religion, upon womanly dignity, sobriety, and purity, upon manly patriotism, was the result of brooding not upon abstract ethics, but upon the immediate necessities of the community. But the stern insistence upon these virtues, which elevated them from mere rules of expediency into authoritative ideals, did more than merely preserve the community. It secured its progress. Pure families sent forth disciplined men into senate and battlefield. The increase of the citizens in number and power flowed from and yet also stimulated the qualities which made the growth of civic organisation possible. Where men can be trusted, progress is inevitable. Trustworthiness is the deepest fact in God; it is the root of all movement towards an ideal, alike in Himself and in His intelligent creatures. In that little city of Rome men could be trusted as husbands, as fathers, as sons, as soldiers, as rulers; and that central moral condition led them to cherish various detailed virtues and to meet the demands for faithful service which prosperity and growth made upon them.

When we speak, then, of character as the root and secret of social progress, we must think, first, of the possession of high moral ideals, and, secondly, of personal loyalty in their pursuit; the citizens accept certain virtues as of binding authority, and can depend on one another to aim at their fulfilment. When that mutual confidence begins to disappear, throughout large sections of a community, decay sets in.

Few if any thinkers would now dispute the assertion that religion has been always vitally connected with social morality. All efforts to imagine mankind in a pre-religious condition are failures; and hence all efforts to describe the rise of a social state without the influence of religion are equally futile. The fact is, as Kaftan has well put it, "The question as to the historical origin of religion is inseparable from those others which deal with the beginnings of the human race or with the origin of all that which, like speech and morality and objective knowledge, is along with religion distinctive of man."[1] You can as soon conceive mankind speechless as irreligious. Various attempts have been recently made to describe the exact function which religion exerts in the social organism. Every one feels, as Professor Huxley did,[2] the difficulty of accounting for the transition from the almost pure individualism of the animal state to the moral life of mankind. The cosmic process demands that the individual organism shall maintain its own existence; human society demands that a man shall sacrifice his pleasure and even sometimes his life for others. Spinoza tried in vain to deduce all practical ethics from that root, the striving to maintain one's own existence; and no one since his day has done any better. But how do we pass from the one to the other? More and more widely it is being seen that the bridge from the self-centred life of the animal to the social morality of man has been built by faith in supernatural powers, and is for ever pillared upon religious experience. The fact is described in different ways according to the method of approach, but the agreement of

[1] *Das Wesen der Religion*, 2nd ed., p. 20.
[2] Cf. quotation above, p. 233.

thinkers upon this matter is growing more and more impressive.[1]

Whatever may be the defects of Mr. Benjamin Kidd's definition of religion, or of his curious, but not inexplicable, use of the term "ultra-rational," he has certainly described the function of religion in the development of society in a most suggestive manner. Religion has stood, as it were, between individual impulse and social obligation, curbing the former and quickening the latter. The former is the spring of all conduct, and, if unregulated, would lead only to selfish action; but impulse is regulated by the demands of law or of social obligation, and this is supported by the authority of the powers who are worshipped, whether in faith or in fear. However crudely some religions have expressed the essential element of this religious instinct, that which seems common to them all, so far as they have become forces in society, has been that sense of responsibility to some power which is above both the individual, whose impulses stir him to selfish action, and society, which demands that he shall live for it. Manifestly, the higher conception of that power which is over both the individual and his social environment, will lead to a higher conception of

[1] For example, compare with Mr. Kidd's form of statement what Bagehot says when speaking of law as "the primary want of mankind": "To gain that obedience, the primary condition is the identity—not the union, but the sameness—of what we now call 'Church' and 'State.' The king must be priest and prophet-king—the two must say the same because they are the same." —*Works* (American ed.), vol. iv., p. 440.

the mutual relations of the members of society. It is here that we must look for the deepest explanation of the varied effects produced by the religions of the world. That which any people believed the supreme powers to be, has been one of the main roots of their history and of their place in civilisation. And yet, as Robertson Smith pointed out in a very striking passage, all heathen religions have failed to reach the conception of supernal powers that possessed a *fixed* as well as a noble or ideal character.[1] A Greek or a Roman god or goddess might represent or idealise a certain virtue, but that had little or no *force* in compelling obedience to that virtue. In fact, Rome had never so many altars to deified virtues, as in the period of her decay. The higher the place of a deity in the hierarchy of heaven, the more vague and unmeaning was his character. Surrounded with loftier dignity, clothed with the majesty of physical power or superhuman wisdom he might be; but his moral nature, where it was not evil, was at least indistinct, and exercised little or no influence upon the actual motives of men.

Here we meet one of the most difficult problems in the history of religion. There can be no doubt that religion has been a moulding force, has acted beneficially in providing some kind of sanction for those tribal and national customs which, however crude or far from a true morality, yet seem to maintain order and lay the foundation of civilisation : on the other hand, we find that throughout

[1] *The Prophets of Israel*, 2nd ed., p. 66.

the heathen world the deities which have been at any period most profoundly worshipped, whether in faith or in fear, have reflected the current morality of the people. That there has been action and reaction between the character of the people and the character of their deities is evident. How to state the terms of that mutual influence is the delicate task.

But now, in the religion of revelation, we find that the two fundamental requisites, which no other religion has been able to describe even as ideals with any approach to fulness and accuracy, are fulfilled. On the one hand, the object of Christian faith is a Being who is manifested as at once holy and loving. He has a character which we dare not judge, because it judges all men, which we cannot praise except in worship, whose vision has given the world a new morality, a new hope, and is giving individual men a new heart. On the other hand, this Being, the living God, is manifested as seeking and securing the fellowship of men. All heathen attempts at worship, at prayer, at incantation or at prophecy, at philosophic scrutiny of the Highest Good, or at mystic absorption in the thought of the All, the One, the unchanging Eternal, are at last rebuked and blessed, crowned and cursed. For now God enters into a living intercourse with men in the person of Jesus Christ. The eternal character is revealed, and revealed in the double act of redeeming by a supreme sacrifice and of establishing an eternal fellowship with men. That is Christianity. It is the fulfilment of those instincts which worked in the heart of all religions; and yet it is at the same time the condemnation of all in those religions that was "of sin" and led men into darkness and despair.

We are learning to-day to appreciate more accurately the stages by which this wondrous result has been reached. When we stand with Abraham and behold in his faith the faint beginnings of monotheism; when we trace the growth of that faith through the critical periods of Israel's history; when we realise that here a new phenomenon is before us, namely, a faith which grows purer and stronger, instead of baser and weaker, with the flight of time, one which becomes grander and deeper in its intellectual assertions instead of falling away into the inept, the vague, the puerile, —then the conception of a God who has taken hold of individual men and of man's history assumes an overwhelming authority. When at last we see and watch and prove Jesus Christ, and find that through Him we have a life of intercourse with God, the evidence becomes irresistible that here at last the real relations of mankind to the Eternal are made known, that now a fellowship with God can be experienced which will carry the moral nature of each man forward to its true glory.

In fine, we see in Christianity the ideal of the divine character and the ideal of man's fellowship with God both realised. No man can possibly picture either of these ideals in a fashion which shall surpass the manner in which Jesus Christ has presented them to us,—else were that man a greater

benefactor to the race, a truer Saviour, a more
sublime and convincing personality than Jesus
Himself. The perfect God and the way of man's
ever perfect fellowship with Him! Any whisper
of another destiny or another religion, which the
world may have heard since that revelation was
made, has only been heard to be scorned as poorer,
meaner, less worthy of God and of man, and *therefore*
false. Here religion burning with its intensest
bliss and morality shining with its utmost beauty
are interfused. Here a personal fellowship with
God is not separated from, but inwardly united
with, character. It depends on, it flows from, the
character of God; and it creates in man the image
of the divine, the Christlike character.

But this experience of fellowship with God,
while itself as inscrutable as thought or feeling
or life, can be, and must be, tested in its manifestations. Such an experience, if it be real, can
only be founded upon unique events, propagated
by unique means, and manifested in unique effects,
among the characters and lives of men and of
nations.

In the preceding chapters we have been attempting to watch some of the forces which the Christian
religion is bringing to bear upon the human race
as a whole. We have seen that it alone of all
religions has been able, without the exercise of
physical force or external prestige, to propagate
its life amongst all races and classes of men. We
have seen that, alike in its nature as a religion and
in its actual operation throughout the world, it

alone can claim to be a universal religion. The study of the spread of Christianity during this century has shown us both the means through which, and the manner in which, it is taking hold of the heart and life of humanity. Through the gift of the Scriptures which present a common basis and a supreme standard of religious ideals and experience to all men; through the work of education which this religion has naturally stimulated, and which it finds necessary to its own true life and deepest influence; through the work of transforming individual moral character which Christianity has from the beginning accounted its supreme visible task; through the impulse which it has given to what we call the civilisation of savage races, an impulse which, so far as one can see, they were not receiving, and were not likely to receive, from any other source—through these various instrumentalities Christianity has proved itself a living force of universal significance.

We see this force drawing all nations together through one common faith and worship, through the possession of one moral ideal and one eternal hope. We see it fitting men to sustain the positions of trust in which the growth of civilisation places them. We see it moulding their characters, and so making human progress possible wherever man breathes and this gospel is preached. In fact, this force has been, before the eyes of this generation and on a scale unequalled in history, acting as the principal cause of that which we all feel to be a reality, and which we rejoice in as " the progress of man."

There are four features connected with the spread of the Christian faith in heathendom, which seem to need special remark in their relation to the progress of which we have been speaking.

It has been said by Mr. Herbert Spencer in describing the " Theological Bias," [1] that the Christian man who is a theologian is apt to pass over " the proofs found everywhere, that a people is no more capable of suddenly receiving a higher form of religion than it is capable of suddenly receiving a higher form of government ; and that inevitably with such religion, as with such government, there will go on a degradation which presently reduces it to one differing but nominally from its predecessor." One feels tempted to enter a vigorous denial that proofs of that last affirmation are " found everywhere." Undoubtedly the proof may be " found everywhere " that many converts from heathenism to Christianity do not honourably adorn the doctrine of the New Testament. We have already dealt with the fact that in the general loosening from old sanctions and customs some moral disasters take place. It no doubt does happen that the profession of the white man's religion is felt by many to give them a kind of social prestige, and so exalts them unduly in their own eyes. The very association of an intimate and confidential kind which the converts enjoy with the white man tends to create in some conceit,

[1] *The Study of Sociology*, p. 301.

laziness, and selfishness. But these phenomena are not unparalleled in the New Testament descriptions of the life of the early church. It must also be admitted that when a community of fresh converts is left too soon to manage its own affairs, the spirit and methods of management will sometimes contain elements that are ignorant and heathen. The general aspect of such a community might seem to casual observers to " differ but nominally from " what preceded. But there is another side to the question. That which is fatally wrong in Mr. Spencer's assertion is the implication that " the degradation " he refers to is final. It is no such thing. Nowhere in the missionary field, so far as I have heard, is the character of Christian converts persistently declining. On the contrary, it is everywhere persistently advancing. Out of the first, the inevitable, moral confusion and intellectual errors, the converts are passing into a clearer life and loftier apprehensions of the truth.

There are enemies of the Christian faith, and some of them even exponents of evolutionary philosophy, who, when they deal with the truth or untruth of Christianity, argue from premises that are quite unworthy of evolutionists. They appear to assume that if Christianity be true, if the Spirit of Christ be the very power of God Himself, then the social effects of the Spirit ought to be sudden, catastrophic, miraculous. They do not seem to be able to conceive of Christianity as the appearing in history of the latest evolutionary force, whose task it is to take up and use for its own characteristic ends the material presented in human nature as it previously existed, unredeemed and unreconciled with God.

We have found in the preceding chapters ample ground for the opinion that the action of the Christian religion in and upon the history of the race may be truly described as an evolutionary influence. It is true that Christianity affirms the connection of every man thus influenced with God Himself, and there are those who have so poor a conception both of God and the universe, not to speak of the conditions of evolution, as to imagine that the presupposition of direct personal contact between God and human beings would destroy the reality of the evolutionary process. Nevertheless, when we concentrate our attention upon the work of the Christian religion, comparing its influence upon the progress of man with the influence exercised by other religions, and studying its relation to these, the history of the missionary movement, of the self-propagation of the Christian religion in our century, will be found capable of analysis and description like any other aspect or element of social evolution. The inflow of European civilisation upon the vast territories of North America provides us on every hand with interesting illustrations of these phenomena. One can look out upon wide prairie regions which a few years ago were covered with wild grasses and dense forests, but which to-day are ploughed, and sown with grain, and dotted over with villages and cities. The present aspect is as unlike the former as could be conceived. And yet there has been no break in the operation of the principle of continuity. All may seem strange, and even in some aspects supernatural, to the wondering gaze of an aboriginal Indian. At first he may have thought the white man a god and his powers derived from other worlds. He was only ignorant of the extent of the relations of the North American continent and of the possibilities lying buried in the soil under his feet. So it is with the relations of the Christian religion to the soil of heathendom, indeed of universal humanity. There it finds rank grasses, jungles of superstition and horror. But it comes to the soil with a new seed, and, behold its power! Amongst peoples who only seemed capable of idolatry and witchcraft, and into whose minds the thought of a high morality hardly entered, it has proved itself capable of producing the fairest fruits of pureness and love, of honour and self-sacrifice. Just as in North America new crops supplant the old, new kinds of buildings and means of transport take the place of the Indian wigwam and canoe so does the student observer see this universal religion take the place of the other religions of the world. It does so, just because in the struggle for existence it proves itself more capable than these, its competitors, of fulfilling those functions which are peculiar to religion in the development of the nature and history of man.

We have seen why it is that the earlier and ruder conditions of society must give way as soon as progress begins. Destruction is, in nature,

16

always the accompaniment of upbuilding. The new displaces the old. The heightening of the ideal of personal comfort or of social relationship will heighten the ideals of personal character; the latter again tend to call forth greater exertions of self-control. While in this manner the sense of personal inadequacy and moral failure may be deepened, the hope of a better self is set before the individual and becomes a spiritual energy.

This is what the Christian religion would seem to have been doing before the eyes of this century. It is apparently unable to meet with a race which proves itself entirely incapable of social redemption. True, we hear very frequently of so-called "decadent races." Even a writer so moderate and careful as M. Elisée Reclus has said: "One tribe is in full course of progressive evolution, another in incontestable decay."[1] This appears to mean that there are certain races whose moral and social condition is of such a nature that they are being gradually destroyed from the face of the earth. Or it may mean, as we sometimes hear it expressed, that a race has lost its vital energy and is for that reason dying out. This "vital energy" is one of those abstractions which occupy so much place in loose thinking, and are used to fill up so many of the lacunæ in our knowledge, but which do not really help to clear thought or solid conclusions. As a matter of fact, the races which are disappearing are doing so, either, as in Greenland, through the enormous diminution of the population by

[1] *Contemporary Review*, Dec. 1896, art. "Progress," p. 764.

epidemic diseases, or, as among certain South
African tribes and more evidently in the case of
the Australian and New Zealand aborigines, by the
destructive assault of peoples possessed of superior
weapons of war; or, as in the case of some tribes,
through the spread of European vices, which are
extremely fatal in their effects amongst such
people, on account of their ignorance and the
simplicity of their past experience. But over
against the so-called decadence, which one would
rather call the destruction of these races, one must
place the change which is being produced upon
certain tribes which were once in their position or
even undergoing "decadence." There are, for
example, hill tribes in India which undoubtedly
were conquered and driven to the hills by races
superior in warlike methods. Their refuge in the
highlands was probably the sole cause of their
deliverance from destruction. These hill tribes,
having now come in contact with Christianity, give
promise of manifesting an energy and vitality quite
inconsistent with the theory of their decadence
or the exhaustion of their blood. A few years of
rum-selling and of contact with traders and sailors
would have probably swept the inhabitants of
Tierra del Fuego out of existence. But Christian
civilisation has begun to take hold of them, and has
wrought a change so marvellous as to have elicited
the admiration of Charles Darwin, and that famous
annual subscription of five pounds to the society
working amongst them. The North American
Indians were no doubt "decadent" one hundred

years ago. But since they were protected from
the ravages of rum and the tricks of unscrupulous
dealers, and are becoming amenable to Christian
education, they have increased steadily in numbers.
It is time that the word "decadent" were used
with more discrimination regarding the causes
which work the destruction of a people and the
forces which may intervene to prevent it.

By large numbers it is taken for granted that
the goal of human history will be reached in
this world. Many who know better, yet allow
themselves to put most emphasis upon the prospect
of an age when, amid things seen and temporal,
mankind will be perfected. They do this chiefly
for purposes of practical exhortation. Accordingly
we have many dreams of the time when the
relations of each to all will be in perfect equipoise,
when the outward and the inward life of every
man will be in ideal harmony. It would not be
impossible to present arguments of considerable
force against the theory that man has a right to
picture his heaven upon earth, or to picture the
time when his descendants will at last stand perfect
amid a perfected race under these skies. It may
be said that, as of our spiritual ancestors, so of our
successors, they without us shall not be made perfect.

On the one hand, we have the very clear assertions
of science that the present structure of our world
cannot last for ever. Few facts have been borne in
upon the minds of many agnostics with more
dismal effect than this, that visible, physical
evolution must have a distant but definite and

CHRISTIANITY AND THE PROGRESS OF MAN   245

inevitable end. Professor Huxley in his Romanes Lecture said: "The theory of evolution encourages no millennial anticipations. If, for millions of years, our globe has taken the upward road, yet, some time, the summit will be reached and the downward route will be commenced. The most daring imagination will hardly venture upon the suggestion that the power and the intelligence of man can ever arrest the procession of the great year."[1] The note of cheer which the famous lecturer tried to infuse into the sentences which follow that passage was not reassuring. His assurance that we may still have much to live for does not dispel our conviction that even his strong heart needed to rouse itself with much energy from the gloomy depression of that prospect. Men can hardly believe with their whole heart that the race is doomed to extinction, and yet live as if the future were all bright. A Huxley might have the courage to say that we must work for such progress as is possible while we may. The ordinary citizen will feel that the very meaning of progress is destroyed, and that the inspiration has gone from life. Despair about the destiny of the race will stop progress; it will send man back to the life of brutes that perish in a brutal scheme of things.

But to my mind the most startling fact about this conception of a heaven on earth is, that it has never received the sanction of any religion. No religion,—and of course philosophical theories and ethical aspirations of individual men are excluded

_____
[1] *Evolution and Ethics*, p. 85.

246 CHRISTIANITY AND THE PROGRESS OF MAN

from this assertion,—no religion which has taken hold of the hearts of men and ruled them, and which has given powerful impulses to human progress, has ever pictured the ideal condition of man as being attainable in this world. All religions look forward into the future. Not even of Buddhism can it be said that it presents an ideal of human progress without the vision of a future life or with the vision of an earthly bliss; for while it is true that it refuses to consider the continuance of conscious life as anything but a disaster, it refuses also for that very reason to present any picture of a social ideal. For the Buddhist the end of all things is to escape self-consciousness; and towards that his best energies are directed.

As we have said before, that which nearly all religions, and certainly those which have been most influential in the history of society, have more or less dimly foreshadowed, has been some kind of contact between mankind and a power or powers conceived of as supreme. The ideal implied in this yearning of man's prophetic heart came to fullest light in Judaism and to fulfilment in Christianity, namely, a life of perfected personal relations with the living God through His Revealer and our Saviour. But nowhere is it suggested in the New Testament that the aim of Christ was to perfect mankind here; the whole of His own teaching, and certainly the entire religious experience of the apostles, refute such a notion. "Our citizenship is in heaven," said Paul, and he lived from and for that assurance. "It is not yet manifested what we shall be," said John, and he lived by the hope, set on Him who was his ideal of personal pureness. Even the doctrine of the Kingdom, which many describe as if the Saviour had limited it to this world, is tantalising for the very fact that at times it shimmers between heaven and earth, and at times is concerned wholly with the life which is to come. It is never altogether an institution of this world.

The history of modern missions proves that to-day, as in the first century, the newborn hope of a future glory, which is personally assured to the Christian heart, exerts an enormous power over the present life. No more shallow criticism of Christianity could be made, none which ignores facts more amazingly, than that the intense hope of heaven weakens the service of man upon the earth. A psychological theorist might show some strong reasons for expecting such a result, but the universal experience of the Christian church disproves it. When the love and hope of heaven are real and potent over the saint's imagination, then he begins to pray, "Thy will be done on earth even as it is done in heaven"; and when men mean that prayer, they begin to work for its realisation. The loss of that vision of a sphere, where the divine will is universally obeyed, makes it less possible for men to cherish in their hearts a burning desire to see that will realised among men. The loss of that infinite future casts gloom upon earth. The fading of the Christian hope is the paralysis of altruism. Indeed, a dim heaven makes all prayer less full of interest and significance.

It is not easy for theoretical critics of Christianity to realise how and why it is that this faith, which at heart lives on the hope of a future life, has done so much for this world. They easily slip over the fact, which will bear the deepest and most thorough scrutiny, that it is love which unites the cherishing of that hope with the most arduous labour for the visible betterment of human conditions. It is always love which labours. The faith which confers the purest love as a living force upon the hearts of men must be, and is, the mightiest influence known to history.

However, while Christianity does not and cannot tell men to expect the realisation of humanity's ideal in this life, yet the spirit which it infuses into man {has given him the power to take the longest strides of which record can be found towards that very consummation.

The fact is that we see, and are in the midst of, a universe which is all in the making. If any part of nature had reached repose, had attained her ideal, there might be ground for the expectation or the longing that man may share in that perfection here and now. On the contrary, everything is in movement; we think it is a movement forwards. The visible and the present is not the whole fact. We are surrounded on every hand with manifest failures, with prophecies rather than attainments of the ideal, with suggestions of the perfect beauty and truth which nature does not fulfil in anything which is seen. Religion, therefore, is to be judged in the light of this fact, that the heart of man has never felt the present form of human history to be that on which the highest hopes could be centred. We must not ask more of religion than she professes to accomplish, nor of the Christian religion that she should fulfil a function which in her heart of hearts she passionately repudiates, viz., to give man bliss in this world. That which Christianity professes to be is a power that can lead humanity towards its ideal in the eternal world, and there to reach the perfect man. Her power to do that is essentially bound up with her power to manifest the main outlines and qualities of that life, at least in their moral aspects, even amidst the imperfect conditions of the present. If man is made for an immortal life, if in some future state of existence all the generations that have been and all that are yet to pass through this world, shall meet face to face in the marvellous communion of an eternal experience, then the above is all that the ideal religion ought to do. It is all that the Christian religion professes to do.

Now the purpose of the preceding chapters has been to deal with a few sections of the evidence which can be offered in support of the claims of Christianity to be the final religion. The spread of the gospel of Jesus Christ through the heathen world has afforded illustrations of a most remarkable, vivid, and impressive nature, of the power which this religion possesses. This power it has manifested, first, by gradually removing and probably making impossible any other form of religion. The day seems to be not far distant, as we have seen, when the peoples of India and China, not to mention other and smaller lands, will have lost their confidence in the forms of worship which they have hitherto practised and in the beliefs which have nourished that practice. No less clearly has the Christian religion manifested its extraordinary power of seizing those depths of human nature which those other religions had only imperfectly controlled, of actually, visibly raising mankind, making the race move onwards towards loftier ideals of personal and of social life.

But this approximate realisation of the ideal is made possible by the Christian religion, according to its own teaching, only as it is able to bring men *now* into actual, conscious, personal fellowship with God through Jesus Christ. It is true that within the range of the Church there have been many and serious divergencies of statement regarding this life of fellowship with God. We may emphasise, for example, the distinction between Latin Christianity and the doctrine of the Evangelical Churches,[1] where disagreements of the most startling nature will be found. Nevertheless, a glance into the higher devotional literature of the Roman Church, even in this century, will prove that to the whole of Christendom the experience of a present and conscious fellowship with God constitutes the essence of Christianity.[2] Disputation regarding

---

[1] Cf. *Social Evolution*, by Benjamin Kidd (pop. ed.), p. 319.

[2] A young missionary from Africa closed an address before the Royal Geographical Society by saying : "The one reason for my

some of the means and manifestations of that fellowship leaves much common ground between these great sections of Christendom.

The consciousness of fellowship with God is the heart of this religion. Without that all its doctrines and precepts lose either their meaning or their efficacy, or both. It is the intense personal realisation of contact with God Himself, which, according to their own testimony has sent out all those thousands of foreign missionaries into the fields of heathendom, and which has stimulated tens of thousands of men and women in the home-land to follow them with their sympathies, their prayers, oftentimes their tears, as well as with material sustenance. Further, the missionaries have found that into this experience of a fellow-ship with God, identical in nature with their own and with that which was attained by the apostles, multitudes of heathen men and women and children are now entering. They are not cut off from it by the poverty of their past religious conceptions or the abundance of their past vicious habits, by the subtilty of their national mind or the utter crude-ness of their previous thought. They may be all mistaken, of course, but the fact remains that this religious movement is to-day spreading throughout the world by arresting individual cannibals, or Brahmins or negroes or Chinese, as apostles of old were arrested, and as all the scholars and saints of

success in Africa was the reality of the presence and power of God with me night and day."—*The Gospel Message*, by R. N. Cust, LL.D., p. 81.

Christendom have been arrested and brought into the divine life. Moreover, we have seen that the experience of this relationship with God begins to transform character, and as character is transformed, civilisation makes progress amongst all peoples. It is a gradual work, of course. The miracle is not wrought in a moment. This force works, like all others, in time. Converts are not often turned into saints even in a decade. Vices are not quenched throughout the Christian communities which are being formed. All that need be proved, as well as all that can be proved, is that astounding progress is being made; and that the Christian religion is at the root of it all. But at the root of the Christian religion, when it becomes implanted in heathen soil, is the experience of fellowship with God. Without that, the Christian religion would be powerless in the opinion of all those who know best its nature and possibilities.

Christianity is to-day creating this inward relationship to God, and its resulting manifestations of a purer heart and a nobler will, on a scale unparalleled in its own history, and not only unapproached but undreamed of in the history of any other religion.

CONCLUSION

THE task of the man who has made up his mind that Christianity is false, and who would fain establish his judgment by scientific means, is, to prove that this widespread experience of personal fellowship with God is unreal. Or, to put it otherwise, he must aim at proving that one of the main factors of evolution has been a baseless fabric of man's imagination called religion, that an age-long cause of progress has been only a miserable misbelief. If this problem were presented in any other range of human experience, the hostile investigator would find himself compelled to establish one or other of two alternatives. First, he must prove if he can that the alleged object of faith does not exist, and hence that fellowship with God is not the supreme cause of human progress; or, secondly, that the phenomena of Christian experience, associated in the minds of their subjects with that one Cause, can be adequately explained by other causes. It would not be easy, of course, to prove that God does not exist. As the Christian world unanimously attributes its experience to the working of His Spirit, and as the attempt has been made times without number to attack the reality of His existence, we may take for granted that no man of our day, desirous of the reputation of possessing a sober mind, would attempt that task.

There remains, then, only the alternative. And surely it is not too much to ask that those who feel it their duty to attack Christian beliefs, should in some thorough and scholarly fashion present us with a scientific explanation, not only of man's religious experience as a whole, but of the religious experience of Christendom,—an explanation which ignores God. The spread of this religion, as described in these pages, affords an opportunity for scientific investigation at first hand which must be considered of inestimable value. Is religion but the foam on the surface of the river of human history? Is Christianity just the last result of the dreams and the superstitions of the affrighted childhood of human history? Can these or similar positions be adequately or scientifically expounded and defended in the light of the phenomena presented by the missionary movement in the nineteenth century?

In view of all this, it seems not too much to say that this movement, when fully studied in all its power and extent, when seen to be intimately connected with and to complete the deepest aspirations of the human heart, and to exercise in a transcendent fashion the permanent functions of religion; when seen to be full of the richest and most glorious blessings to mankind; and, lastly, when found to be dependent upon and to flow from an alleged fellowship with God, through Jesus Christ, leaves us with only one or other of two conclusions.—Either, the whole movement is a self-deception, grounded on folly; or, the man who studies it is looking into the very mind and heart of the living God.

www.ingramcontent.com/pod-product-compliance
Lightning Source LLC
Chambersburg PA
CBHW031427020726

47499CB00005B/1632

9783337026615